Suppers & Snacks

DAVID & CHARLES

Newton Abbot London

Suppers & snacks.—(David & Charles Kitchen Workshop)
  1. Suppers
  I. Smaretter. *English*
  641.5'3   TX738

ISBN 0-7153-8460-0

© Illustrations: A/S Hjemmet 1980
   Text: David & Charles 1983

Filmset by MS Filmsetting Limited, Frome, Somerset
and printed in The Netherlands
by Smeets Offset BV, Weert
for David & Charles (Publishers) Limited
Brunel House, Newton Abbot, Devon

Suppers and Snacks

As the title indicates, this book contains a large variety of dishes suitable for those occasions when something tasty – but fairly small – is required. They range from ideas for Sunday breakfast for the family, to impromptu and delicious snacks for unexpected guests. If you follow our store-cupboard suggestions, and our recipes, you need never again bemoan the fact that 'there's nothing in the house to eat'!

Quantities to Use
The quantities given in these recipes are generally smaller than in main course recipes, as food such as this is usually served when nobody is exactly starving. It is therefore important to give some thought as to when you are going to serve the dish, how long it is since the last meal, and to judge the portions accordingly. The very young, for instance, adore snacks, tending to eat a little at a time, but often, and they *can* have huge appetites!

The Practicalities
With each recipe we give a rough estimate of the time needed to prepare the relevant dish, and how long it will take to cook. These times can only *be* approximate, as it all depends on the quality of your raw materials, their size, the type of cooking pans you use, as well as the thermostat of your oven.
We have also indicated the oven temperature and where to place the dish in the oven when necessary, and whether or not the dish, or parts of it, can be frozen. This last is of especial relevance to those who like to prepare well in advance, to have a snack meal virtually ready for any unexpected occasion, only requiring defrosting.

Your Store-cupboard
Snacks and suppers do not require an enormous amount of preparation, and you do not have to buy in huge quantities of food. The essence of this sort of catering is to have an efficient store-cupboard – which includes your refrigerator and freezer – even if the stored item is only required to add that final touch.

It is always to your advantage to have a good basic stock of products that will keep, either in cans or bags, etc, whether stored in your cupboard, larder, refrigerator or freezer. We have detailed what we think you should stock, as well as a rough guide to fresh ingredients. Many of you may think these listings too comprehensive, but choose what *you* think *you* need and will use the most, and stock up again as soon as your shelves empty. It's a good idea to write the date bought on *all* goods in your store-cupboard and freezer, to use the older products first, and to keep a close watch on the products which already have a date-stamp marked on them.

Food in Cans or Jars
Fish/Shellfish Tuna fish, mackerel, sardines, cod roe, anchovies, shrimps, crab meat, mussels, lumpfish roe and pilchards.
Vegetables Tomatoes, asparagus, mushrooms, tomato purée, sweetcorn, beansprouts, broad or green beans, pickled peppers, onions, gherkins and beetroot.
Soup Tomato, asparagus, spinach, chicken, consommé, beef, fish and shellfish.
Meat Ham, beef, meat balls, pâté, sausages, pies and main course dishes.
Fruit Peaches, apricots, pineapple, mandarins, mixed fruit salad, pears, and perhaps some special treats like figs or cherries. Various kinds of jellies, jams and marmalade.
NOTE: Remember to store certain jars and cans – lumpfish roe etc – in the refrigerator, as well as any you have opened and not used up. Some jars and cans are date-stamped and

must be used by that date. If cans start to bulge, the contents are fermenting, and must never be eaten. If the date-stamp is still valid, take them back to the shop where you bought them.

Other Groceries
Various kinds of flour, pasta, rice, oats, dried peas, beans, lentils, coffee, tea, cocoa, brown and white sugars, various seeds, oil, vinegar, juices and squashes, raisins, prunes and other dried fruits, various nuts. You can also store gravy powder, stock cubes, mustard, and sauces such as soy, Worcestershire, chili and tomato ketchup.

Fresh Vegetables, Herbs and Fruit
Potatoes, onion, garlic, celery, carrots, leeks, cabbage, peppers, cucumber, tomatoes, mushrooms and some variety of lettuce. Broccoli, spinach, green beans, peas, radishes, parsley, chives, cress, dill, and seasonal fresh fruit. Many of these need to be kept in the refrigerator.

Spices and Dried Herbs
Nearly everything needs to be seasoned to taste with spices and/or herbs. The following ought to be in your store-cupboard at all times: household salt and sea salt, black and white peppercorns, curry powder, nutmeg, paprika, onion and garlic salt, cinnamon, ginger and mixed spice; bay leaves, marjoram, oregano, thyme, rosemary, basil, tarragon etc.
NOTE: Ready-ground spices and dried herbs are easier to use, but fresh are always better. Remember that dried herbs have twice as much

flavour as fresh, so use half the quantity if dried. Store herbs and spices in a dark, dry place in tightly closed jars or containers.

Bread
Bread needs to be bought frequently, but in the interests of taste and variety, try different kinds – white, brown, flat Greek bread, French loaves, pumpernickel, rye – or you can make your own (see pages 54–7 for some recipes).

Egg and Dairy Products
Eggs, milk, butter, double, single and sour cream, yoghurt, cream cheese, cottage cheese, various cheeses good for cooking and garnishing (Cheddar, Gruyère, Emmenthal, Parmesan etc).

Frozen Goods
Peas, green beans, Brussels sprouts, spinach, broccoli, or various kinds of mixed vegetables; bacon, minced meat, chicken, chops, steaks, hamburgers etc; whole or filleted fish, fish fingers, shrimps and other shellfish; ready-made complete dishes, home-made or bought. It is always useful to have things like home-made stocks, soups and sauces in the freezer.

Left-overs
Left-over meat, fish and vegetables can be used in many small dishes, combined with fresh ingredients. We therefore mention left-overs in some of the recipes. Always remember though, to cool left-overs quickly, and store well wrapped, or in jars or boxes with tight-fitting lids, in the refrigerator or in the freezer.

A large lattice (vol-au-vent) filled with chicken and mushrooms makes a delicious supper, a good starter, or a nice buffet table dish.

Lattice Vol-au-Vent

1 Roll out the pastry and cut two 12–15cm (5–6in) diameter circles. Place one on a baking sheet.

2 Make a large hole in the other circle and fasten to the first circle with egg white and cocktail sticks.

3 Cut strips from the rest of the pastry, and make a lattice lid to fit. Bake separately.

Pastry Savouries

Lattice Vol-au-Vent
(serves 6)
Preparation time: about 20 min
Cooking time: about 30 min in all
Oven temperature: 200–220°C, 400–425°F, Gas 6–7
Suitable for the freezer

450–700g (1–1½lb) frozen puff pastry
1 egg, separated, for glazing

1 Defrost the pastry. Roll out on your working surface to make a fairly thin rectangle, rolling one side only at a time. Cut out one circle, 12–15cm (5–6in) in diameter, and place on baking sheet.
2 Roll out the remaining pastry, and cut out another circle of the same dimension. Cut out a hole, leaving a 2–3cm (1–1½in) broad ring. Brush the outer edge of the base with lightly whisked egg white and place the ring on top.
3 Trace or cut out narrow strips from the pastry remaining to make a lattice top. Leave everything in a cool place for about 15 min.
4 Brush with whisked egg, making sure that none of the egg runs down the sides. You should only brush the top surfaces, otherwise the pastry will rise unevenly.
5 Bake base on the bottom rack of the oven for 15–20 min, and the lid for 10–15 min.
Fill the vol-au-vent (see separate recipe) and serve immediately, to prevent the base going soft.

Individual Vol-au-Vents
(serves 8)
Use about 250g (9oz) defrosted puff pastry. Roll out and cut out 16 rounds. Cut 8 of them into rings by using a smaller glass. Brush the whole pastry bases with egg white and place rings on top. Brush rings on top as well, not letting any of the egg run down the sides (this would make the vol-au-vents lopsided during baking). Bake bases and their lids (the small circles remaining after cutting out the rings) on a baking sheet, covered in baking paper, at a very high temperature

Individual Vol-au-Vents, with asparagus added to the filling, make excellent starters.

(240°C, 475°F, Gas 9) until golden and nicely risen. Remove carefully from baking sheet. Add ½ portion vol-au-vent filling. Place lids on top.

Vol-au-Vent Filling
Preparation time: about 20 min
Cooking time: 45–60 min
Suitable for the freezer

1 large chicken
salt, whole black peppercorns
1 bouquet garni (see method)
about 100g (4oz) butter
2 × 15ml tbsp (2 tbsp) plain flour
100–200ml (4–7fl oz) double cream
250g (9oz) mushrooms
1 lemon

1 Place chicken in a saucepan and pour water on top. Bring to the boil and skim well.
2 Add 1 × 5ml tbsp (1 tbsp) salt, 4–5 whole black peppercorns and a bouquet garni made from 1 leek, 1 stalk of celery and ½ sprig of parsley. Allow to boil for about 45 min or until meat is tender.
3 Remove skin and bones and slice meat into small pieces. Boil stock for a while without the lid, and strain.
4 Melt 25–40g (1–1½oz) butter in a saucepan. Stir in flour and dilute with warm stock until you have a smooth, thick sauce. Allow to boil for a few minutes and add cream and extra seasoning to taste.
5 Clean mushrooms, slice, and sauté in the remaining butter with the lemon juice. Add meat and mushrooms to the sauce and mix carefully.

Ham Croissants (above)
(makes 9–12)
Preparation time: about 20 min
Cooking time: about 15 min
Oven temperature: 200–220°C,
400–425°F, Gas 6–7
Unsuitable for the freezer

*about 400g (14oz) frozen puff
  pastry*
50g (2oz) butter
2 shallots or small onions
*about 200g (7oz) cooked ham,
  coarsely chopped*
1 sprig of parsley, finely chopped
2 eggs, beaten
salt, pepper, nutmeg
1 × 5ml tsp (1 tsp) English mustard

1 Defrost pastry. Clean and finely
chop the onion and sauté in butter
for 6–8 min. Turn off heat and add
ham, chopped parsley and beaten
eggs (but leave some of the egg for
brushing). Season with salt, pepper,
nutmeg and mustard.
2 Roll out pastry and cut into 20cm
(8in) squares. Cut each square in
half to form 2 triangles. Place one
spoonful of stuffing on each triangle,
and roll up from the broad side
towards the point. Bend croissants
slightly into a half moon shape and
place on a dampened baking sheet.
Brush croissants with remaining
beaten egg, and bake until crisp and
golden on the middle rack of the
oven. Serve with a green salad.

Sausage Rolls (right above)
(makes 16–20)
Preparation time: about 15 min
Baking time: 12–15 min
Oven temperature: 200–220°C,
400–425°F, Gas 6–7

about 200g (7oz) frozen puff pastry
*1–2 × 15ml tbsp (1–2 tbsp) made
  mustard*
350–400g (12–14oz) sausages
egg, for glazing

1 Defrost pastry, roll out and
cut into strips long enough and
wide enough to wrap around your
sausages.

2. Brush a thin layer of mustard on
the pastry strips and wrap round the
sausages, pressing the ends together
lengthwise with a little water.
3 Place sausages on a dampened
baking sheet, cut ends down (or
cover sheet with baking paper).
Make a few incisions in the pastry
and brush with beaten egg. Bake
until pastry is crisp and golden in
the middle of the oven. Serve with a
green salad.

Savoury Pasties (right below)
(makes 12–20)
Preparation time: 10–20 min
Cooking time: about 15 min
Oven temperature: 200–220°C,
400–425°F, Gas 6–7
Unsuitable for the freezer

*about 200g (7oz) frozen puff or
  flaky pastry*
*1–2 × 15ml tbsp (1–2tbsp) made
  mustard*
*350–400g (12–14oz) filling (see
  below)*
egg for glazing

1 Defrost pastry and roll out thinly. Cut out rounds, small or large according to taste, and spread thinly with mustard (optional). Place one spoonful of stuffing on the middle of each round. Brush the edges with egg or water and fold in the middle to make a half moon shape. Press edges tightly together.

2 Shape pastry into small fish if using a fish or shellfish stuffing. Cut out double the amount of fish shapes (use a cardboard template). Place two fish together, with the stuffing in the middle. Brush edges with egg and squeeze tightly together.

3 Place pasties or fish on a baking sheet, dampened, or covered with baking paper. Make a few incisions in the dough with a sharp knife and brush with beaten egg. Bake until crisp and golden in the middle of the oven.

Serve pasties hot with a green salad.

Anchovy Stuffing

2 chopped, hard-boiled eggs mixed with 1 small can well drained chopped anchovy fillets, 1 finely chopped stalk of celery, 1 × 15ml tbsp (1tbsp) mayonnaise, 1 × 15ml tbsp (1tbsp) chopped capers and a touch of finely chopped dill.

Chicken Stuffing

Cut about 225g (8oz) cooked chicken (boneless) into small cubes and mix with 100g (4oz) crisply fried, crushed bacon, 2–3 × 15ml tbsp (2–3tbsp) tomato purée, salt, pepper, and parsley or basil.

Fish/Shellfish Stuffing

About 225g (8oz) cooked boneless fish in small bits mixed with about 100g (4oz) mussels or shrimps and 50g (2oz) boiled or defrosted, frozen peas. Mix together 1–2 × 15ml tbsp (1–2tbsp) mayonnaise with a touch of lemon juice, grated onion, salt, pepper, finely chopped tarragon and dill and mix fish, shellfish and peas into the sauce.

Egg and Ham Stuffing

Mix together 2–3 × 15ml tbsp (2–3tbsp) mayonnaise, lemon juice to taste, a touch of curry powder, salt, pepper and finely chopped cress. Add 3 hard-boiled chopped eggs and 100–150g (4–5oz) cooked, chopped ham or pork.

Above: Supper Platter. Right: Weekend Salad. Below: Roast Beef with Marinated Cauliflower.

Cold Supper Snacks

Weekend Salad
(serves 4)
Preparation time: about 15 min
Unsuitable for the freezer

a cooked chicken
100–225g (¼–½lb) mushrooms
½ cucumber
1 lemon
1 can beansprouts (or about 100g or
 ¼lb fresh)
4 ripe tomatoes
1 small jar stuffed olives
For the dressing : 1 × 15ml tbsp
 (1tbsp) white wine vinegar
salt, pepper
2 × 5ml tsp (2tsp) French mustard
4–5 × 15ml tbsp (4–5tbsp) oil

1 Bone and skin the chicken, and
slice meat into pieces. Wash and
trim mushrooms, slice, and sprinkle
with lemon juice.
2 Rinse beansprouts under cold,
running water. Wash tomatoes and
cucumber and slice.
3 Mix all ingredients in a salad
bowl. Mix the dressing ingredients
together and sprinkle over the salad.
Serve with warm French bread.

Supper Platter
Serve a delicious and visually temp-
ting supper by presenting a variety
of things on one plate. Arrange sardines, liver paté, ham, cod roe and a
bit of cheese on one plate. Garnish
with lettuce leaves, lemon, lumpfish
roe and radishes.

Marinated Cauliflower
(serves 4)
Preparation time: about 15 min
Marinating time: about 1 hr

1 small cauliflower
1 × 15ml tbsp (1tbsp) white wine
 vinegar
salt, pepper
2 × 15ml tbsp (2tbsp) capers
4 × 15ml tbsp (4tbsp) oil

1 Wash and clean the cauliflower
well and divide into tiny flowerets.
Cook until barely tender in lightly
salted water. Drain well.
3 Mix a marinade of vinegar, salt,
pepper, capers and oil and pour over
the cauliflower. Marinate for about
1 hr.

Tuna Fish Salad (left)

(serves 4)
Preparation time: about 20 min
Unsuitable for the freezer

75–175g (3–6oz) macaroni (or
    other tubular pasta)
salt, pepper
1 iceberg or other crisp lettuce
4 tomatoes
1–2 cans tuna fish in oil
2–4 hard-boiled eggs
50–100g (2–4oz) black olives
For the dressing: 2 × 15ml tbsp
    (2tbsp) white wine vinegar
1 clove of garlic
4–5 × 15ml tbsp (4–5tbsp) olive oil
parsley, dill, tarragon

1 Boil pasta until al dente, and rinse under cold water. Rinse lettuce leaves.
2 Pour oil off tuna fish and flake fish into smaller pieces. Slice tomatoes and eggs into wedges.
3 Cover bottom and sides of a large bowl with lettuce leaves. Mix all the other ingredients carefully together and add to the bowl. Mix the dressing and pour over the salad.
Serve with French bread and butter.

Bacon Salad

(serves 4)
Preparation time: about 15 min
Unsuitable for the freezer

about 300g (11oz) green beans
    (fresh, tinned or frozen)
100–150g (4–5oz) thin bacon
    rashers
2 hard-boiled eggs
salt, pepper
about 100g (4oz) mushrooms
2 × 15ml tbsp (2tbsp) lemon juice
1–2 shallots or small onions
3–4 × 15ml tbsp (3–4tbsp) oil

1 Cook the green beans until barely tender in lightly salted water (heat canned beans in their stock). Mix a dressing of lemon juice, salt, pepper, grated or finely chopped onion and oil and sprinkle on top of the warm beans. Leave to cool.
2 Cut bacon into strips, fry until golden and drain on kitchen paper. Cut the hard-boiled eggs in half, remove the yolk and place to one side. Chop the whites coarsely. Slice the cleaned mushrooms.
3 Mix egg whites and mushrooms into the beans and sprinkle the

bacon bits on top. Squeeze egg yolks through a sieve and sprinkle on top of the salad.
Serve freshly made with French bread or toast.

Cheese Salad (below)

(serves 4)
Preparation time: about 15 min
Unsuitable for the freezer

75–175g (3–6oz) macaroni (or
    other tubular pasta)
salt
3–4 small tomatoes
2 hard-boiled eggs
1 bunch radishes
pepper
100–150g (4–5oz) Gruyère,
    Emmenthal or Cheddar

50g (2oz) good quality cream cheese
lemon juice
cream
finely chopped dill or chives

1 Boil pasta until al dente, drain and rinse under cold, running water.
2 Slice eggs, tomatoes and radishes, and mix them with small cheese cubes in the salad bowl.
3 Beat cream cheese and stir until smooth with lemon juice and a touch of cream. Season dressing to taste with salt, pepper and 2–3 × 15ml tbsp (2–3tbsp) finely chopped dill or chives. Pour dressing over salad and leave in a cold place for about 15 min before serving.
Serve with bread and butter.

Fondues

Serving a fondue is a delightful way of entertaining, not least because everyone cooks their own food! A heavy flame-proof casserole dish will do if you don't possess a special fondue pot.

Meat Fondue
(serves 6)
Preparation time: about 1 hr

450g (1lb) tender, well-hung beef
  (rump, sirloin or fillet)
For the meat balls:
400–450g (14–16oz) lean beef,
  mince
1 onion
1 egg
oil, salt, pepper
about 750ml (1½pt) good quality
  vegetable oil
Accompaniments: see recipes

1 Prepare accompaniments in advance. Green and red sauces can be made a day in advance and left in a cold place until ready to use. Cube the meat just before serving. Mix together the mince, grated onion, egg, 2–3 × 15ml tbsp (2–3tbsp) oil, salt and pepper. Shape into medium meatballs.
2 Heat oil on top of the cooker first, and then move the fondue pot onto a stand with a spirit flame underneath. Make sure the pot is standing securely on the stand, and always have a lid handy to extinguish the flames if the oil should ignite.
3 Each guest helps himself to meat or meatballs, piercing it with a long fondue fork, and cooks it himself in the hot oil. Serve a selection of accompaniments and seasonings on the table around the fondue pot.

Red Sauce
Finely chop 1 onion, 1 small leek or 2 stalks of celery. Sauté in 3 × 15ml tbsp (3tbsp) oil and add 200ml (7fl oz) tomato purée, 1 shredded bay leaf, ½ × 5ml tsp (½tsp) dried thyme, ½ × 5ml tsp (½tsp) dried basil, salt and black pepper to taste. Allow to simmer on low heat for about ½ hr, stirring from time to time, and finally add 200ml (7fl oz) strong red wine. Serve hot or cold.

15

Green Sauce

Mix together 200g (7oz) mayonnaise and 100ml (4fl oz) milk or plain yoghurt, 1 sprig chopped parsley, dill or chives (or a mixture of all three) and 1 crushed garlic clove. Season to taste with lemon juice, salt and pepper.

Other Accompaniments

Pommes frites or oven chips
Pickled gherkins
Grated horseradish or horseradish cream
Black or green olives
Lettuce, cress
Raw mushroom slices in lemon juice
Tomato wedges, peeled and dressed with oil and vinegar
Capers or pickled pearl onions
Coarse sea salt and pepper in a grinder

Fish Fondue (below)

(serves 6)
Preparation time: about 1 hr in all

about 450g (1lb) plaice fillets
For the marinade: 3 × 15ml tbsp
(3tbsp) lemon juice
3 × 15ml tbsp (3tbsp) oil, 5 sprigs of
parsley
1 red pepper
salt
a pinch of cayenne pepper
For the fondue: 250ml (9fl oz) olive
oil
250g (9oz) shallots or small onions
salt
3 carrots
½ bulb fennel
1 can tomatoes
pepper
1 clove of garlic
marjoram or oregano

4–5 × 15ml tbsp (4–5tbsp) tomato
purée
100–200ml (4–7fl oz) dry vermouth

1 Mix together all the ingredients for the marinade. Rinse and dry plaice fillets well. Slice fillets into bite-sized pieces and leave in marinade for about ½ hr.
2 Finely chop the onions and fennel and grate the carrots. Sauté everything in oil for about 10 min on low heat. Add tomatoes and juice from tin and leave everything to simmer for 40–50 min. Season with crushed garlic, tomato purée, herbs and dry vermouth.
3 Place fondue pot with the tomato fondue sauce on a stand with a spirit flame underneath. Pierce fish slices with long fondue forks and cook in the hot sauce for a few minutes.
Serve the following accompaniments with your fish fondue: 300g (11oz) unpeeled shrimps
200g (7oz) crawfish tails or scampi
1–2 bulbs of fennel, sliced in wedges, and steamed, and garlic bread (see page 19).

Fondue with Smoked Pork

(right)
(serves 6)
Preparation time: about 45 min

about 1kg (2¼lb) boneless smoked
pork loin, or gammon
1 bottle dry white wine
2–4 cloves of garlic
5 whole black peppercorns
1 × 15ml tbsp (1tbsp) fresh or
1 × 5ml tsp (1tsp) dried thyme
2 × 15ml tbsp (2tbsp) fresh or
2 × 5ml tsp (2tsp) dried basil
For the accompaniments: 1 portion
tomato sauce (as for Fish Fondue)
1 portion Green Sauce (see above)
about 200 ml (7fl oz) sour cream
250g (9oz) sliced mushrooms in oil
and lemon marinade
½ iceberg or other crisp lettuce,
shredded, with oil and vinegar
dressing
2 French loaves

1 Prepare the accompaniments and place in dishes. Place pork or gammon on a breadboard with a good, sharp knife next to it.
2 Heat the white wine to boiling point along with crushed or chopped garlic, peppercorns and finely chopped or crushed herbs. Place fondue pot above spirit flame.

3 Slice pork or gammon very thinly, roll up, and pierce with fondue fork. Dip the meat in the wine for a few seconds (it only needs to heat through, not cook).
Serve with accompaniments and hot loaves.

Shellfish Fondue (left)
(serves 6)
Preparation time: about 45 min

400g (14oz) large shrimps
200–300g (7–11oz) cooked crab
* claws, scampi or something similar*
1kg (2¼lb) fresh mussels, steamed, or
* 1 large can mussels*
250g (9oz) mushrooms
For the fondue: shrimp shells and
* heads*
2 × 15ml tbsp (2tbsp) oil
40g (1½oz) butter
200ml (7fl oz) dry white wine
200–300ml (7–10fl oz) fish stock
2 cans whole tomatoes
1 clove of garlic, salt
cayenne pepper or chili sauce
For the accompaniments: 1 portion
* Green Sauce (see page 16)*
2 French loaves
lime or lemons

1 Peel shrimps and set aside. Crush shell and heads and sauté in butter and oil. Add wine, and fish stock or liquid from mussel can. Simmer for about 20 min on low heat. Strain the stock and squeeze all liquid from the shrimp shells and heads.
2 Cook for a further ½ hr together with tomatoes and their juices, crushed garlic and spices until you have a smooth, thick sauce. Pour this into the fondue pot and place on stand over a spirit flame.
3 Place peeled shellfish and mushrooms on fondue prongs and heat in fondue. Serve with French loaf, Green Sauce, and halved lemons squeezed over the warm shellfish.

Cheese Fondue (right)
(serves 6)
Preparation time: about 30 min

1 clove of garlic
300–400ml (½–¾pt) dry white wine
400–450g (14–16oz) Gruyère cheese
200g (7oz) Cheddar cheese
½ lemon
2 × 5ml tsp (2tsp) cornflour
50ml (2fl oz) Kirsch, gin or vodka

white pepper, nutmeg
½ × 5ml tsp (½tsp) bicarbonate of
* soda*
For the accompaniments: white
* bread, butter and garlic*

1 Rub fondue pot on the inside with a crushed garlic clove and pour in the wine. Grate cheese coarsely and add to the pot with the lemon juice. Heat until cheese melts, stirring every now and again.
2 Mix cornflour with the spirit and stir into the simmering cheese. Season with spices and stir in bicarbonate of soda.
3 Sauté cubes of the day-old white

bread briefly in garlicky butter. Each guest pierces a cube with a fork, dips it in the melted cheese, and eats it immediately.

Garlic Bread
Make a deep cut along the whole length of a French loaf (don't cut it right through). Mix together 100g (4oz) soft butter, 2–3 × 15ml tbsp (2–3tbsp) finely chopped parsley, 1–2 crushed garlic cloves, a dash of salt and pepper. Spread mixture along the cut and heat bread in oven (at about 200°C, 400°F, Gas 6) for about 5 min. Cut loaf into small slices or chunks.

Light and Delicious

Make small hot dishes from fresh or canned mussels, canned crab and sardines. Served with bread and salad, they turn a snack into a meal.

Steamed Mussels

(serves 6)
Preparation time: 15–20 min
Cooking time: 5–8 min
Unsuitable for the freezer

about 2kg (4½lb) fresh mussels
50g (2oz) butter
2 shallots or small onions
1 clove of garlic
1 carrot
1 stalk of celery
3 sprigs of parsley
1 bay leaf
1 sprig of thyme
400ml (¾pt) dry white wine
salt, whole black peppercorns

1 Mussels must be fresh, heavy and undamaged. Scrub well in cold, running water. Discard any mussels which do not close when you tap the shell lightly.
2 Melt butter in a large pot and add chopped onion, crushed garlic, grated carrot, finely sliced celery, herbs and white wine. Bring everything to the boil. Add a pinch of salt, 6–8 peppercorns and then the mussels. Boil vigorously with the lid on. Shake the pot often.
Mussels which do not open after boiling for 6–8 min must be discarded.
3 Remove mussels from pot with a slotted spoon, along with some of the vegetables and spices, and place in a bowl. Boil stock for a little longer, and then pour over mussels through a sieve lined with a well wrung-out cloth. Serve piping hot in soup dishes with warm, crisp French bread.
NOTE: 2kg (4½lb) fresh mussels can be replaced by about 450g (1lb) canned mussels.

Far left : Mussels au Gratin and Mussel Fritters
At the back : Steamed Mussels
In the front : Mussel Gratin (see recipe on the following page).

Mussel Fritters

(serves 6)
Preparation time: about 20 min
Cooking time: about 10 min in all
Unsuitable for the freezer

about 2kg (4½lb) steamed mussels
1 egg + 1 egg yolk
breadcrumbs
oil or lard

1 Remove mussel meat from shells and turn first in whisked egg and egg yolk, then in breadcrumbs. Leave to dry for a while. Heat oil or lard in a wide saucepan or chip pan.
2 Place 6–8 mussels at a time in the fat and deep-fry until golden brown. Drain on kitchen paper.
Serve hot with tartare sauce.

Tartare Sauce

Mix 150g (5oz) mayonnaise with 1 × 15ml tbsp (1tbsp) lemon juice, 1–2 × 5ml tsp (1–2tsp) light, French mustard, 2 × 15ml tbsp (2tbsp) small capers, 3–4 chopped pickled gherkins and a sprinkling of finely chopped tarragon or parsley.

Mussels au Gratin

(serves 6)
Preparation time: 20–25 min
Cooking time: about 15 min in all
Unsuitable for the freezer

about 2kg (4½lb) steamed mussels
15g (½oz) butter
1 × 15ml tbsp (1tbsp) flour
150–200ml (5–7fl oz) mussel stock
100ml (4fl oz) double cream
2 egg yolks
salt, pepper, lemon juice
breadcrumbs
about 50g (2oz) grated Parmesan cheese and Gruyère cheese, mixed

1 Place steamed mussels in shell halves on a large ovenproof dish.
2 Simmer butter and flour on low heat, dilute with mussel stock and stir on the boil for a few minutes. Add egg yolks whisked together with cream.
Keep sauce warm, but do not allow to boil. Season with salt, pepper and lemon juice.
3 Sprinkle each of the shells with a little sauce and sprinkle with grated cheese mixed with 1–2 × 15ml tbsp (1–2tbsp) breadcrumbs. Bake in a very hot oven (240°C, 475°F, Gas 9) until surface is golden.

Mussel Gratin

(serves 6)
Preparation time: about 20 min
Cooking time: approx. 35 min in all
Oven temperature: 200–220°C, 400–425°F, Gas 6–7
Unsuitable for the freezer

about 2kg (4½lb) steamed mussels
*   (or large can mussels)*
2 shallots or small onions
25g (1oz) butter
100g (4oz) mushrooms
3 × 15ml tbsp (3tbsp) plain flour
250ml (9fl oz) stock from mussels or
*   brine from can + water*
250ml (9fl oz) single cream
2 eggs, separated
100g (4oz) grated Gruyère cheese
salt, pepper
paprika
3 × 15ml tbsp (3tbsp) grated
*   Parmesan cheese*

1 Remove mussel meat from shells and strain stock through a sieve lined with a clean damp cloth, or through a coffee paper filter.
2 Chop up onions and mushrooms and sauté until golden in butter. Stir in flour, leave to simmer for a short while, and then stir in stock and cream. Remove sauce from heat, stir in grated cheese and egg yolks and season.
3 Whisk egg whites until stiff and fold into sauce. Spread half the sauce over the bottom of a greased ovenproof dish, place mussels on top and cover with remaining sauce. Sprinkle with cheese and paprika and bake in the bottom of the hot oven for about 20 min.
Serve with bread and butter.

Warm Crab Salad (below)

(serves 5–6)
Preparation time: about 15 min
Cooking time: a few minutes at 250°C, 475°F, Gas 9
Unsuitable for the freezer

2 onions, 1 green pepper
1 clove of garlic
40g (1½oz) butter
2 × 15ml tbsp (2tbsp) chopped
*   parsley*
2 × 15ml tbsp (2tbsp) breadcrumbs
1 raw egg
3 hard-boiled eggs
wine vinegar, chili sauce
salt, pepper
paprika
1 large or 2 small tins crab meat

1 Sauté peeled, chopped onions and pepper, crushed garlic and chopped parsley gently in butter in a covered pan for 6–8 min.
2 Turn off heat and stir in breadcrumbs, beaten egg and chopped hard-boiled eggs. Season with wine vinegar, chili sauce and spices. The mixture should have a sharp flavour.
3 Clean crab meat, remove any small bones and cut into smaller pieces. Mix crab meat carefully into spicy egg mixture.
4 Divide crab salad between scallop shells or individual ovenproof ramekins, and place in the hot oven, or under a hot grill, until dishes are heated through, and golden.

Tomato Sardines (right)

(serves 5–6)
Preparation time: about 15 min
Cooking time: a few min. at 240°C, 475°F, Gas 9
Unsuitable for the freezer

2–3 cans of sardines in oil
3–4 × 15ml tbsp (3–4tbsp) tomato
*   purée*
1 onion, 1 clove of garlic
4 × 15ml tbsp (4tbsp) oil, paprika
salt, cayenne pepper
100ml (4fl oz) double cream
horseradish (finely grated or cream)
250g (9oz) mushrooms
1 lemon, 1 sprig of parsley

1 Brush scallop shells or individual ovenproof dishes with a little oil from the sardines and place 2–3 well-drained sardines in each.
2 Mix tomato purée with 2 × 15ml tbsp (2tbsp) oil, 1–2 × 15ml tbsp (1–2tbsp) lemon juice, grated onion, crushed garlic, spices, lightly whipped cream and horseradish. The sauce should have a strong spicy flavour, but go easy on the cayenne pepper. Its strong flavour increases with heating.
3 Divide sauce over the sardines and place shells or dishes in the hot oven until heated through. Meanwhile clean mushrooms. Cut into slices and turn immediately in a marinade of lemon juice, oil, salt and chopped parsley.
Serve sardines straight from the oven with white bread and marinated mushrooms, and a salad of shredded cabbage and mandarin wedges dipped in lemon juice is a good accompaniment.

Fishy Feasts

Norwegian Pickled Herring
(right)
(serves 4–6)
Preparation time: about 30 min
Marinating time: at least 24 hrs
Cooking time (for accompaniments): 20–30 min
Unsuitable for the freezer

8–10 herring (fresh, rollmop,
   Bismarck, or salt) fillets
2–3 onions
For the pickling brine: 150ml ($\frac{1}{4}$pt)
   white wine vinegar
150ml ($\frac{1}{4}$pt) water
100–150g (4–5oz) sugar
$1\frac{1}{2} \times 5$ml tsp ($1\frac{1}{2}$tsp) whole allspice
   berries
a few white peppercorns
1 bay leaf
For the accompaniments: 700–900g
   ($1\frac{1}{2}$–2lb) new potatoes
300–400g (11–14oz) green beans
1 onion
100g (4oz) bacon, dill

1 If using fresh herring, scale and wash, and cut away the heads and tails. Slit down the belly, clean, and gently pull backbone and any other small bones away. If using salt herring, soak for 24 hours before filleting.
2 Peel the onions and slice into rings. Stir sugar in vinegar and cold water. Add coarsely crushed allspice berries, white peppercorns and bay leaf.
3 Place herring fillets and onion rings in layers in a large jar and pour pickling vinegar over. Leave in a cold place for at least 24 hrs (preferably 2–4 days).
4 For the accompaniments, boil potatoes in their jackets, with a generous handful of dill. Simmer beans in lightly salted water.
5 Chop up the onion and slice bacon into cubes and sauté until golden. Serve herring on ice, garnished with dill. Leave beans to drain well and serve with bacon and onion on top. Potatoes boiled with dill are a must with this dish.

Tomato Herring
(serves 4–6)
Preparation time: about 15 min
Marinating time: 2–3 hrs
Unsuitable for the freezer

6–8 pickled herring fillets (rollmop
   or Bismarck)
4 ripe tomatoes
salt, pepper, paprika
2 onions
3 × 15ml tbsp (3tbsp) capers
1 small can tomato purée
100ml (4fl oz) red wine or tomato
   juice
wine vinegar
salt
cress or dill to garnish

1 Soak herring fillets if necessary. Slice into bits.
2 Wash tomatoes and slice. Sprinkle with a pinch of salt, pepper and paprika. Place tomato slices in layers with herring pieces, onion rings and capers in a jar or a bowl.
3 Mix together tomato purée and red wine or tomato juice and season with a touch of wine vinegar, paprika and salt. Pour marinade over herring and leave for at least 3 hrs. Garnish with cress or dill.

Left: Apple Herring. Right:
Anchovy Temptation.

Apple Herring
(serves 4–6)
Preparation time: 10–15 min
Marinating time: about 12 hrs
Unsuitable for the freezer

6–8 herring fillets (fresh, rollmop,
   Bismarck or salt)
2 onions
   2–3 apples
200–300ml (7–10fl oz) sour cream
made mustard
white wine vinegar

1 For preparation of fresh or salt herring, see previous recipe. If the fillets are too salty, they should be left to soak in water and milk for a few hours. Slice fillets into fairly big pieces and place in an earthenware or glass jar.
2 Peel onions and slice into rings. Wash apples, remove core and cut into bits. Place onion and apples in the jar.
3 Mix together sour cream and a dash of mustard and add wine vinegar to taste. Pour over herring.

Anchovy Temptation
(serves 4)
Preparation time: 10–15 min
Cooking time: 20–30 min
Oven temperature: 200°C, 400°F, Gas 6
Unsuitable for the freezer

about 1kg (2¼lb) firm potatoes,
   boiled in their skins
2–3 onions, salt, pepper
75–100g (3–4oz) butter
250ml (9fl oz) single cream
1–2 small cans of anchovies
milk (optional)
4 egg yolks

1 Peel potatoes and slice them. Peel onions and cut into rings.
2 Place potatoes, onion, thin slices of butter and half of the anchovy fillets in layers in dish. Season.
3 Pour cream over and cover dish with tinfoil for the first 10–15 min. Dilute with milk if necessary. Bake on the middle shelf of the oven.
4 Top with the rest of the anchovy fillets and egg yolks in their shells.

25

Smoked Fishy Feasts

Smoked Fish and Scrambled Eggs with Cheese

(serves 4)
Preparation time: about 20 min
Cooking time: 3–4 min
Unsuitable for the freezer

4 large slices of white bread
50–75g (2–3oz) butter
4–6 eggs
100ml (4fl oz) single cream
salt, pepper
100g (4oz) grated cheese
smoked fish (herring, mackerel,
* trout, eel or salmon)*
1 bunch of chives

1 Remove skin and bones from fish and place fillets to one side.
2 Fry white bread slices until golden in about half the butter. Keep warm.
3 Beat eggs lightly together with cream and pour mixture into pan with the remaining butter, melted. Allow egg mixture to set on low heat. Scrape along the bottom with a wooden spatula or spoon. Mix in grated cheese when the egg mixture has thickened, and turn off heat. Season to taste with salt and pepper.
4 Divide scrambled eggs between the hot bread slices and place smoked fish fillets on top. Sprinkle with chives and serve immediately.

Smoked Herring with Egg

(serves 4)
Preparation time: 15–20 min
Unsuitable for freezer

4 large slices of white bread or crisp
* bread*
butter
lettuce leaves
lemon juice
2 small onions
4–6 smoked herring, trout or
* mackerel*
4 egg yolks

1 Butter bread slices and place washed lettuce leaves on top. Sprinkle lettuce with a little lemon juice. Peel onions and cut into thin slices.
2 Clean the smoked fish. Remove as many small bones as possible. Place 2–3 fillets on each bread slice and place $\frac{1}{2}$ egg shell with the raw egg yolk on top of each. Serve immediately.

Raw egg yolk is always a good accompaniment for smoked fish. There are endless possibilities for extra garnishes : bread, butter, lettuce, finely chopped radishes, onion rings or chopped onion, capers and chives.

Smoked Mackerel on Spinach
(serves 4)
Preparation time : about 20 min
Cooking time : about 5 min
Unsuitable for the freezer

1 large or 2 small smoked mackerel
450g (1lb) fresh or 1 large packet
  frozen spinach
about 75g (3oz) butter
½ lemon
50g (2oz) fresh cream cheese
salt, pepper, nutmeg
4 eggs
1 small French loaf or 4 slices of
  square white bread

1 Clean mackerel carefully, and remove all skin and small bones. Rinse fresh spinach well in cold water or place frozen spinach in a colander to defrost.
2 Place mackerel fillets on a large piece of tinfoil with 15g (½oz) butter and sprinkle with lemon juice. Fold tinfoil around the fish, not too tightly. Place packet in a dry frying pan and heat mackerel on low heat, turning the packet several times.
3 Boil eggs for 5–6 min. Remove shell and halve.
4 Steam drained spinach 2–3 min in 15–25g (½–1oz) butter. Add cheese and stir until melted. Season. Fry sliced bread in remaining butter, adding more if necessary.
5 Place spinach in a hot serving dish and place warm mackerel fillets and halved boiled eggs on top.
Serve immediately with fried bread or toast.

Smoked Buckling Platter
(serves 4)
Preparation time : about 20 min
Cooking time : about 10 min
Oven temperature : 220°C, 425°F, Gas 7
Unsuitable for the freezer

6 buckling
2 onions
1 sprig of dill
150ml (¼pt) single cream
1 × 15ml tbsp (1tbsp) mustard

1 Grease an ovenproof dish and line with sliced onions and ½ of the finely chopped dill. Clean and fillet the buckling and place fillets on top.
2 Mix cream with mustard and pour over fish. Bake as indicated and sprinkle the rest of the dill over as you serve.
Boiled or baked potatoes and a green salad are the best accompaniments.

The Versatile Potato

The potato is probably the most familiar vegetable, appearing at family meals at least once a day. The following recipes demonstrate the potato's adaptability and versatility.

Potato Nests

(makes 8–10)
Preparation time: about 30 min
Cooking time: 12–15 min
Oven temperature: 220°C, 425°F, Gas 7
Unsuitable for the freezer

For the potato purée: 1kg (2¼lb)
   mealy potatoes
50g (2oz) butter
50g (2oz) cream cheese
3 egg yolks
salt, white pepper
nutmeg
a little cream (optional)

1 Peel potatoes, cut into small bits and boil until tender in water without salt. Pour off water and steam potatoes until dry. Push through a sieve or use a potato masher.
2 Stir in butter, cheese, 2 egg yolks and seasonings, whip until fluffy. Add a little cream if too dry.
3 Pour mash into a piping bag and form round "nests" on a well-greased baking sheet or baking paper. Brush nests carefully with a further ½ egg yolk whisked in 1 × 15ml tbsp (1tbsp) water. Bake as indicated in the middle of the oven. Serve potato nests warm or cold, depending on the filling.

Ideas for Fillings:

● Mixed vegetable salad with a dressing of cottage cheese, seasoned with lemon juice and spices.
● Cooked chicken with mushrooms, asparagus and finely chopped cress, mixed with mayonnaise and a touch of cream.
● Cold, sliced roast beef with gherkins, grated horseradish cream and a little tartare sauce.

Left: Warm or cold Potato Nests can be filled with lots of delicious fillings.

● Braised peas, carrots and small onions, sprinkled with chopped ham.
● Cooked chicken, asparagus and mushrooms in a light sauce.
● Left-over dark, strong beef or game stew, with carrots.
● Mince sauce with onion, celery, tomatoes and spices.

Stuffed Baked Potatoes

(serves 4)
Preparation time: 10–20 min
Cooking time: 60–75 min
Oven temperature: 200–240°C, 400–475°F, Gas 6–9
Unsuitable for the freezer

4 large mealy potatoes
oil, salt

1 Scrub, rinse and dry potatoes well. Brush with oil.
2 Make an incision in the top of the potatoes, wrap them in tinfoil and place on a baking sheet or in an ovenproof dish.
Time of cooking varies depending on size, so test them with a thin needle to see if tender.
3 Fold tinfoil down a bit and squeeze potatoes lightly. The incision will open. Place stuffing inside and serve potatoes piping hot.

Ideas for Stuffings:
Cheese

Mix about 100g (4oz) fresh cream cheese with 50g (2oz) soft butter and 2 × 15ml tbsp (2tbsp) cream. Add 3–4 × 15ml tbsp (3–4tbsp) grated Parmesan cheese and season with lemon juice, paprika, finely chopped chives and a few capers, if you like.

Caviar (Lumpfish Roe)

Mix about 200ml (7fl oz) sour cream with a touch of lemon juice and coarsely ground black pepper. Stir carefully together with a touch of 'caviar' and fill potatoes with this cream.
Place more 'caviar' on top and garnish with dill.

Spiced Butter

Mix 75–100g (3–4oz) soft butter with 1 × 15ml tbsp (1tbsp) lemon juice, 2 × 15ml tbsp (2tbsp) chopped parsley, ½ garlic clove, crushed, white pepper to taste or 2–3 × 15ml tbsp (2–3tbsp) red wine, 1–2 × 5ml tsp (1–2tsp) crushed, green peppercorns, paprika or 1 grated small onion, 1–2 × 5ml tsp (1–2tsp) made mustard, 1 × 5ml tsp (1tsp) wine vinegar, and 4–5 × 15ml tbsp (4–5tbsp) finely chopped chives, cress or parsley.

Below: A baked potato is always tasty, and we give many suggestions for even tastier fillings.

Dishes with Peppers

Green peppers can be used in many different dishes – in hot main courses, in cold salads with tuna fish etc, and can be stuffed in a variety of ways.

Pepper Salad

(serves 6)
Preparation time: about 15 min
Unsuitable for the freezer

2–3 green peppers
4 tomatoes
4 pickled gherkins
2 shallots or small onions
1 can tuna fish in oil
1 can mussels
salt, pepper
1 lemon
chives

1 Cut each of the rinsed peppers in four, lengthways. Remove seeds and white membrane.
2 Scald and peel tomatoes. Cut tomatoes, gherkins and peeled onions into small bits and strips.
3 Sauté together in the oil from tuna fish can, lemon juice, salt, pepper and finely chopped chives. Mix tomatoes, gherkins, onions, tuna fish and well-drained mussels on a serving dish. Sprinkle with the oil and lemon juice mixture and arrange pepper slices around the edge.

Stuffed Green Peppers

(serves 4)
Preparation time: 15–20 min
Cooking time: 20–25 min in all
Suitable for the freezer, but will lose flavour.

4 green peppers
50g (2oz) bacon, 1–2 onions
250g (9oz) mince (pork or beef)
1 slice crustless white bread
½ can tomatoes
10–12 stuffed olives (optional)
salt, pepper
paprika
basil, sage
1 small can tomato purée
100ml (4fl oz) cream

1 Wash peppers, cut off a lid at the stem end, and remove seeds and inner membranes. Simmer peppers and lids in lightly salted water for about 5 min. and drain.
2 Fry small bacon cubes in a large, deep, lidded pan until the fat runs. Add chopped onions and mince and brown everything on strong heat, stirring continuously.
3 Stir in crumbled white bread, well-drained tomatoes and chopped olives (if used), and season with salt, pepper, paprika and fresh or dried herbs. Divide mixture between peppers, pushing it well in.
4 Add juice from tomatoes and tomato purée to the pan, place the stuffed peppers in this, and put their lids on. Cover the pan. Simmer for 10–15 min., then remove the peppers and keep warm. Allow tomato sauce to simmer for a while longer, and stir in the cream. Season the sauce, return peppers to the pan, and serve immediately.
Boiled rice and a salad go well with stuffed peppers.

Peppers with Ham and Eggs

(serves 4)
Preparation time: 15–20 min
Cooking time: 10–15 min
Unsuitable for the freezer

2 large, round green peppers
150g (5oz) cooked ham
150g (5oz) mushrooms
½ lemon
small sprig of parsley
15g (½oz) butter
salt, pepper
4 eggs
100–200ml (4–7fl oz) chicken stock

1 Cut the rinsed peppers in two, slice off top and bottom, clean and steam for a couple of min. in butter in a lidded pan.
2 Sprinkle cleaned sliced mushrooms with lemon and mix with chopped ham and finely chopped parsley. Press stuffing into pepper halves. Add stock and seasonings to pan and steam for a further 10 min. until peppers are tender.
3 Break an egg on top of each pepper half 3–4 min before the end of cooking time, and allow whites to set completely. Garnish with left-over coarsely chopped pepper (from the top and bottom), or chives.

From top, clockwise: Pepper Salad, Stuffed Green Peppers and Peppers with Ham and Eggs.

Vegetables and Stuffings

Tomatoes, pepper and cucumber are good, colourful vegetables which can be used for savoury snacks or for starters. Fill them with a variety of delicious things, and your guests are sure to come back for more.

Stuffed Tomato, Cucumber and Pepper
(serves 4)
Preparation time: about 20 min
Unsuitable for the freezer

4 large tomatoes or 8 small ones or 2 large peppers or 1 medium cucumber

1 Rinse and dry the vegetables:
Tomatoes Cut off a lid and remove the flesh and seeds with a spoon. Sprinkle inside with a pinch of salt and place tomatoes upside down in a sieve.
Cucumbers Slice cucumber in two lengthways and across the middle (so that you have 4 pieces). Scrape out pips and some of the flesh to make room for the stuffing.
Pepper Cut a lid off small peppers at the stem end, and pull out the seeds and membranes. Or you can halve large peppers across, and clean them in the same way.
2 Fill with one of the following stuffings and serve with toast or rolls and butter.

Ideas for Stuffings
Tuna Fish and Rice
Mix 1 can of well-drained tuna fish, flaked, with about 100ml (4fl oz) boiled long-grain rice, 1 coarsely chopped, hard-boiled egg, 1 × 15ml tbsp (1tbsp) mayonnaise with a dash of lemon juice, 6–8 coarsely chopped olives, salt, pepper and 2 × 15ml tbsp (2tbsp) finely chopped tarragon or parsley.

Top to bottom:
Stuffed Tomato with Tuna Fish and Rice. Stuffed Tomato with Spinach and Cheese. Stuffed Tomato with Egg and Herbs.

This stuffing is especially good in tomatoes and cucumber.

Spinach and Cheese
Mix about 450g (1lb) steamed, coarsely chopped spinach with 1 small grated onion and some left-over mince, or crumbled hamburger or sausage etc. Mix in 2 × 15ml tbsp (2tbsp) tomato purée to hold stuffing together, and season with salt and pepper, nutmeg, a couple of drops of soy sauce and finely chopped chives. Slice 50–75g (2–3oz) firm cheese (Cheddar or Gruyère) in thin strips and mix with the stuffing. Suitable for filling tomatoes and cucumber.

Egg and Herbs
Sauté 2–3 thin rashers of bacon, cut into strips, in a small saucepan. Turn off heat and stir in 1 crushed garlic clove, 1 slice crumbled white crustless bread and 2–3 lightly whisked eggs. The mixture should be fairly thick. Add salt, pepper and 3–4 × 15ml tbsp (3–4tbsp) finely chopped mixed herbs (like cress, parsley, chives, tarragon, lemon balm etc). This filling is best for tomatoes or peppers. Bake the tomatoes or peppers for a few minutes in a hot oven after you have filled them.

Cream Cheese with Olives
Mash 100–150g (4–5oz) fresh cream cheese and about 25g (1oz) Stilton or other blue cheese, and stir until smooth with a dash of milk, cream or lemon juice. Season with some finely grated onion and a pinch of cayenne pepper. Mix in 10–12 stuffed olives. Leave to set in refrigerator. This tastes – and looks – marvellous in green peppers when sliced as shown in the top photograph on the facing page.

Cheese Salad with Radishes
Make a light sauce of 50–75g (2–3oz) mayonnaise, about 100ml (4fl oz) sour cream and a dash of lemon juice. Add salt, pepper and a generous amount of finely chopped parsley and some green from celery tops. Mix about 200g (7oz) mild cheese (Dutch is ideal), cut into cubes, and 1–2 finely chopped celery stalks into the sauce. Add some grated radishes, and garnish filled cucumber or tomatoes with thin slices of radish.

Above : Delicious Cheese Cream with Olives in crisp green peppers.

Below : A lightly hollowed out cucumber filled with Cheese Salad, garnished with radishes.

Hot Vegetable Dishes

Tomato and Brussels Sprouts Platter

(serves 4)
Preparation time: 10–15 min
Cooking time: 15 min in all
Suitable for the freezer unbaked

100–150g (4–5oz) bacon
2–3 onions
300g (11oz) Brussels sprouts
200–300ml (7–10fl oz) stock
about 450g (1lb) ripe tomatoes
left-over cooked meat – beef, ham,
   chicken or sausage (optional)
salt, pepper, thyme
marjoram, basil
about 100g (4oz) mild cheese

1 Cut bacon into small cubes and fry until lightly golden in a casserole with coarsely chopped onions.
2 Clean sprouts, add to the casserole and sauté for 2 min. Add stock and boil until tender.

3 Scald and peel tomatoes, cut into wedges and season.
4 Pour everything into a greased ovenproof dish, mix in tomatoes and left-over meat, chicken or sausage (optional). Sprinkle with herbs, and grate cheese on top. Leave dish in a hot oven (220°C, 425°F, Gas 7) until cheese melts.

Tomato and Onion Tart

(serves 6)
Preparation time: 25–30 min
Cooking time: about 1 hr
Oven temperature: 200°C, 400°F, Gas 6
Suitable for the freezer

For the pastry: 200g (7oz) flour
salt
150g (5oz) butter, 1 egg
For the filling: 6 onions
40g (1½oz) butter
salt, rosemary, thyme
1 can tomatoes
paprika, basil
about 200g (7oz) cottage cheese
cream
1 small jar pickled herrings or a can
of anchovies
10 green olives (optional)
parsley, egg for glazing

1 Rub together butter and flour, add ½ × 5ml tsp (½tsp) salt and knead to a dough with the egg. Leave in a cold place.
2 Meanwhile sauté coarsely chopped onions until tender and barely golden in butter, and season to taste with salt and finely chopped herbs. Coarsely chop tomatoes (discard juice) and add salt, paprika and basil. Stir cottage cheese until smooth with a little cream. Pour off the liquid from the herrings or anchovies. Chop olives and parsley.
3 Roll out pastry and place ⅔ in a greased springform tin. Place stuffing in layers in the tin, starting with the onions, then tomatoes, cottage cheese, herring or anchovy pieces, olives and finally parsley.
Roll the remaining pastry to make a lid and cut small holes in it (see right). Fold outer edges of pastry lining over stuffing, brush with whisked egg and place lid on top. Squeeze edges well together, brush with the egg and bake, until pastry is well coloured and crisp.

*Below right:
Tomato and Onion Tart.*

Tomato and Brussels Sprouts Platter, baked with cheese.

Baked Chicory (right)
(serves 4–6)
Preparation time: 15–20 min
Cooking time: about 20 min in all
Unsuitable for the freezer

8 medium heads of chicory
salt, 1 lemon
For the batter: 125–150g (4½–5oz)
    plain flour
2 eggs, salt
about 200ml (7fl oz) beer (non-
    alcoholic or light ale)
oil or lard
parsley

1 Remove any dead outer leaves
from chicory. Cut out stem. Dry
with a cloth.
2 Boil chicory for 8–10 min in
lightly salted water with lemon
juice. Place in a sieve, with the root
upwards, and cool.
3 Mix together a batter of plain
flour, egg yolks, beer and
1–2 × 5ml tsp (1–2tsp) water. Whisk
egg whites until peaks form and fold
into the batter. Heat oil to a temperature of 180–190°C (350–375°F)
in a chip pan.
4 Dip whole chicory in batter and
place 1 or 2 at a time in the chip pan.
Turn them to make sure they turn
nicely golden all round. Drain on
fat-absorbent paper and keep warm.
5 Rinse parsley sprigs and dry
them. Place parsley in the fat and fry
until crisp and dark green. Serve
with bread and wedges of lemon.

Add an Egg

There are many ways of preparing eggs, ranging from the simplest boiled breakfast egg, to the most sophisticated dishes. Here, poached eggs accompany expensive and cheap ingredients to make stunning dishes...

Egg Steaks or Hamburgers
(serves 4)
Preparation time: 5–10 min
Cooking time: 2–3 min
Unsuitable for the freezer

4 small slices steak (rump, sirloin or
   fillet) or 4 fried hamburgers
pepper, salt, butter
4 poached eggs (see next page)
4 slices of white bread
4 × 15ml tbsp (4tbsp) grated
   cheese or breadcrumbs
pickled gherkins
cress, parsley or chives

1 Rub meat slices with coarsely ground black pepper and leave in a cold place. Toast bread and poach the eggs.

2 Fry small steaks for $\frac{1}{2}$–$1\frac{1}{2}$ min on each side in butter, or heat the fried hamburgers well. Sprinkle salt on meat and place on toast in an oven-proof dish. Place eggs on top, sprinkle with grated cheese or breadcrumbs and place dish in the oven (at 240°C, 475°F, Gas 9) or under grill until cheese starts to melt. Sprinkle with finely chopped gherkins, cress, parsley or chives.
A green salad goes well with these tasty little steaks.

VARIATION
Instead of poached eggs, you could use braised fennel, tomato slices, fried onions or tinned fruit. Choose depending on taste, the occasion, or what you have in the larder.

Shrimps with Eggs

(serves 4)
Preparation time: about 15 min
Unsuitable for the freezer

25g (1oz) butter
2 × 15ml tbsp (2tbsp) plain flour
250ml (9fl oz) single cream
salt
grated nutmeg
200g (7oz) peeled shrimps
3 × 15ml tbsp (3tbsp) braised, cubed
  celeriac, celery or fennel
4 eggs, parsley

1 Melt butter, stir in flour and leave
to simmer for a couple of min without going brown. Stir in cream
gradually and stir continuously until
smooth. Season with salt, nutmeg
and finely chopped parsley.
2 Poach the eggs (see following
recipe), and keep warm.
3 Fold celeriac, celery or fennel and
shrimps into the sauce and pour into
a hot dish. Place eggs on top.
Garnish with parsley and serve with
bread and butter.

Kidney with Poached Eggs

(serves 4)
Preparation time: about 20 min
Cooking time: about 2 min in all
Unsuitable for the freezer

1 small calf kidney
plain flour
salt, pepper, butter, vinegar
4 eggs, 2 × 15ml tbsp (2tbsp) parsley
4 slices of white bread
For the sauce: 200ml (7fl oz) light
  stock
1 small can of truffles or about 50g
  (2oz) mushrooms
1 × 5ml tsp (1tsp) tomato purée
1 × 5ml tsp (1tsp) cornflour
2–3 × 15ml tbsp (2–3tbsp) Madeira

1 Cut skin from kidney, halve and
remove central core. Soak in vine-
gary water for about 1 hr, and then
slice. Turn slices in well-seasoned
flour.
2 Heat stock, slice the truffles or
sautéed mushrooms, and put into
the stock. Add tomato purée and
thicken with cornflour mixed with

cold water. Season with Madeira
and a touch of salt and pepper. Keep
sauce warm.
3 *Poached eggs* Bring water to the
boil in a saucepan, add $\frac{1}{2}$–1 × 5ml tsp
($\frac{1}{2}$–1tsp) vinegar and 1 × 5ml tsp
(1tsp) salt. Crack eggs in a cup and
let them slide into saucepan. Collect
the white around the yolk with two
spoons and leave eggs to simmer for
3–4 min. Remove with slotted
spoon and place in a dish of hot
water.
4 Cut bread into slices the same size
as the kidney slices. Fry until golden
in butter and place on a hot serving
dish. Sauté kidneys until brown in
15–25g ($\frac{1}{2}$–1oz) butter on medium
heat. Place on fried bread slices with
poached eggs on top. Pour Madeira
sauce over, sprinkle with parsley
and serve warm with a green salad.

Left: Egg Steaks or Hamburgers.
Below: Kidneys with Poached Eggs,
with fried bread and Madeira sauce.

37

Liver and Horseradish Cream
Fry liver slices as above and place on toast. Top with a horseradish cream, either the proprietary kind, diluted with a little whipped double cream, or 200ml (7fl oz) whipped double cream and 2–3 × 15ml tbsp (2–3tbsp) fresh grated horseradish. Fry 2–3 thin rashers of bacon until crisp, crush and sprinkle on top.

Liver and Cabbage Salad
Fry liver slices as above, and put on toasted bread. Place a salad on top, made from finely shredded white cabbage and a whole berry jam (such as bilberry or whortleberry).

Liver and Mushroom Cream

200g (7oz) mushrooms
1 finely chopped onion
25g (1oz) butter
finely chopped parsley
a pinch of thyme, salt
100–150ml (4–5fl oz) double cream
1–2 × 15ml tbsp (1–2tbsp) plain flour
parsley to garnish

Sauté cleaned, finely chopped mushrooms and onion in butter on low heat. Stir in plain flour and cream. Season with parsley, thyme and salt. Leave to simmer for 15 min, put on top of the liver.

Left: Mini Hamburgers with Spiced Butter.

Tasty Toppings

Amazingly tasty and visually exciting dishes can be concocted from the most economical ingredients with the right garnish and presentation.

Liver and Cheese Toasts
(serves 4)
Preparation time: about 15 min
Cooking time: about 10 min in all
Unsuitable for the freezer

2 slices calves' liver
2–3 onions
25g (1oz) butter
plain flour, salt, black pepper
4 slices square bread
½ red pepper
50g (2oz) fresh cream cheese
15g (½oz) blue cheese
2 × 15ml tbsp (2tbsp) finely chopped cress or parsley

1 Slice peeled onions into thin rings and fry until golden in 15g (½oz) butter. Sprinkle with salt and set aside. Cut pepper into thin rings.
2 Cut liver slices in two, turn in seasoned flour, and fry for about 2 min on either side in the remaining butter.
3 Toast bread and place in an oven-proof dish. Put liver, onion and pepper rings on top. Stir soft cream cheese with blue cheese and cress or parsley, and put a little on top of each liver toast. Bake in a hot oven (240°C, 475°F, Gas 9) or grill until cheese melts.
Serve with a salad.

Piquant Patties

(serves 4)
Preparation time: about 15 min
Cooking time: about 15 min in all
Unsuitable for the freezer

about 300g (11oz) beef mince
2–3 onions
butter
salt, black pepper, thyme
2 tomatoes
4 slices of white bread
small pickled gherkins

1 Fry thin onion rings until brown and crisp in 15g (½oz) butter, sprinkle with salt and leave to one side.
2 Mix mince with 2 finely chopped pickled gherkins, ½ × 5ml tsp (½tsp) coarsely ground pepper and 2 × 5ml tsp (2tsp) finely chopped or ½ × 5ml tsp (½tsp) dried, crushed thyme. Shape 8 small patties, and fry for 1–2 min on both sides in butter on strong heat. Sprinkle with salt.
3 Cut bread slices the same size as the patties and sauté lightly in butter or toast them.
4 Cut tomatoes in slices, season, and place on top of fried or toasted bread. Place patties on top with the onion and a pickled gherkin, fastened with a wooden cocktail stick. Serve immediately with a mixed, raw vegetable salad.

Right : Piquant Patties.
Below : Liver and Cheese Toasts.

Mini Hamburgers with Spiced Butter

(serves 4)
Preparation time: 10–15 min
Cooking time: about 15 min in all
Unsuitable for the freezer

250g (9oz) beef or pork mince
4 slices of French bread
salt, pepper, 1 egg yolk
1–2 shallots or small onions
about 125g (4½oz) butter
1 tomato, 1 clove of garlic
2–3 × 15ml tbsp (2–3tbsp) finely chopped parsley
lemon juice

1 Mix about 100g (4oz) soft butter with crushed garlic, finely chopped ends of the tomato, parsley, 1–2 × 15ml tbsp (1–2tbsp) lemon juice and a pinch of pepper. Place butter on a piece of tinfoil and roll to a sausage shape. Wrap in the foil, and put in the refrigerator.
2 Mix mince lightly with coarsely ground black pepper, egg yolk and grated or finely chopped onions. Do not work the mince too much.
3 Shape into 4 small, thick hamburgers and fry for 2–3 min on both sides in remaining butter on fairly strong heat. Sprinkle with salt and place on toasted bread. Cut the remaining tomato into 4 slices, place for a minute in frying pan, sprinkle with salt and pepper.
Place tomato slices on hamburgers and place a thick slice of the cold spiced butter on top. Serve hamburgers with a shredded raw vegetable salad.

Chicken for Economy and Versatility

Chicken is cheap and good, and can be cooked and presented in many different and exciting ways – and is appreciated by both adults and children!

Chicken and Mushroom Casserole (left)
(serves 6)
Preparation time: about 15 min
Cooking time: 30–45 min
Unsuitable for the freezer

2 small chickens (fresh or frozen)
25g (1oz) butter
1 × 15ml tbsp (1tbsp) olive oil
1 clove of garlic
½ cucumber
300ml (½pt) chicken stock
soy sauce
250g (9oz) mushrooms
½ lemon
1 × 15ml tbsp (1tbsp) cornflour
salt, pepper, parsley

1 Defrost frozen birds slowly in refrigerator. Cut chickens into portions. Dry well and brown in half butter and the oil on a medium heat.
2 Add crushed garlic and thick cucumber slices. Sprinkle with a pinch of salt and pepper and add stock with a couple of drops of soy sauce. Leave dish to simmer for 20–30 min.
3 Sauté cleaned mushrooms in remaining butter, sprinkle with salt and squeeze the juice from ½ lemon on top. Add mushrooms to chicken casserole. Thicken meat juices with cornflour mixed with a little cold stock or water. Season gravy, and sprinkle chopped parsley on top. Serve with a green salad and rice or baked potatoes.

Chicken and Asparagus Pancake (above)
(serves 6–8)
Preparation time: about 30 min
Cooking time: about 30 min in all
Pancakes and filling can be frozen separately

For the pancakes : 150g (5oz) plain flour
2 eggs, salt, 200ml (7fl oz) milk
100ml (4fl oz) double cream
50g (2oz) butter
For the filling : 1 fresh or frozen chicken
about 200g (7oz) chicken or calves' liver
1 large can asparagus (about 450g or 1lb) or fresh
250g (9oz) mushrooms, ½ lemon
butter, plain flour
about 100ml (4fl oz) double cream
salt, pepper, cress, watercress or parsley
brandy or dry sherry

1 Mix together pancake batter ingredients, and fry thin, medium-sized pancakes. Use 6–8 of the pancakes for this dish. Freeze the rest in a stack with greaseproof paper in between (to make them easier to separate).
2 Cut chicken in four and simmer for about 15–20 min in enough water just to cover, with 1 × 5ml tsp (1tsp) salt, a slice of lemon, and a pinch of crushed, dried herbs. Brown sliced liver in 15–25g (½–1oz) butter and sprinkle with salt and pepper.
3 Drain asparagus well, retaining the liquid. If asparagus is in season, use fresh, of course. Peel and boil until barely tender in lightly salted water, and drain well. Sauté cleaned, chopped mushrooms in 15g (½oz) butter and season with salt and lemon juice.
4 Melt 40g (1½oz) butter over low heat, and mix in 2½–3 × 15ml tbsp (2½–3 tbsp) plain flour. Do not let it brown. Dilute with a mixture of the chicken and asparagus stock until sauce is fairly thick. Whisk sauce smooth and allow to boil for a couple of min. Stir in cream and season with salt and pepper, and a couple of drops of brandy or dry sherry.
5 Stir chopped chicken and sliced liver into the sauce and place in layers with asparagus and mushroom in between the hot pancakes. Garnish with cress, watercress or parsley, and see following page for further tips.

Above : A tasty, crisp salad is all you need to accompany Indian Chicken Casserole.

TIPS

The stack of stuffed pancakes can be made in advance and kept warm in the oven on low heat. Put a pancake on top and cover it all with tinfoil.

Grated cheese and butter can be placed on top of pancake stack. Just before serving, put the pancakes into a hot oven until the cheese melts.

Instead of a pancake stack, you can mix asparagus, mushrooms, chicken and liver with most of the sauce and divide between 6–8 pancakes. Roll them up individually and place in a large ovenproof dish. Pour the remaining sauce over the top, sprinkle generously with grated cheese, and leave dish in the hot oven (220–240°C, 425–475°F, Gas 7–9) for about 15 min, until everything is heated through and the cheese slightly golden.

If you prepare the pancakes this way, the dish can be made ready the day before. Store in refrigerator and heat up in the oven.

Indian Chicken Casserole

(serves 4–6)
Preparation time: about 20 min
Cooking time: 35–40 min
Oven temperature: 220°C, 425°F, Gas 7
Suitable for the freezer, but will lose flavour

1 large roasting or boiling chicken
salt, pepper, curry powder, oil
50g (2oz) butter
2 large onions
1 clove of garlic
2 bananas, 50g (2oz) flaked almonds
200g (7oz) long-grain rice
1 litre (1¾pt) stock
parsley

1 Cut chicken into 6–8 pieces. Dry well, rub with salt, pepper and curry powder, and sauté gently in butter and oil, until golden.

2 Sauté coarsely chopped onions and crushed garlic until lightly golden in 3 × 15ml tbsp (3tbsp) oil with 1–2 × 5ml tsp (1–2tsp) curry powder in a flameproof casserole. Peel bananas, slice and mix carefully into the onions, along with the flaked almonds, and place chicken

pieces on top.

3 Put the rice into the casserole around the chicken pieces, and pour warm, well-spiced stock over. Cover the casserole tightly, and place at the foot of the hot oven for about 30 min, or until chicken is tender. Sprinkle with finely chopped parsley when ready. Serve with a green salad.

Chicken Royale

(serves 4)
Preparation time: about 15 min
Cooking time: about 10 min
Suitable for the freezer, but will lose in flavour

1 cooked chicken or chicken left-overs
1 red and 1 green pepper
250g (9oz) mushrooms
salt, pepper, paprika
40g (1½oz) butter
3 × 15ml tbsp (3tbsp) plain flour
400ml (¾pt) chicken stock
100–200ml (4–7fl oz) cream
1 egg yolk

1 Cut boned and skinned chicken into small pieces. Wash peppers, remove seeds and membranes from

inside, and slice into small strips. Clean mushrooms and slice.

2 Sauté pepper and mushrooms for 3–4 min in butter. Sprinkle with flour and dilute with stock to make a smooth sauce. Boil thoroughly for a couple of minutes, stirring continuously. Add egg yolk mixed with cream, sliced meat and seasonings to taste. Keep sauce bubbling until the meat is heated through.

Serve with rice, French bread or rolls with sesame seeds, and a green or beansprout salad.

Baked Chicken Legs

(serves 4)
Preparation time: about 10 min
Cooking time: about 30 min
Oven temperature: 240°C, 475°F, Gas 9
Suitable for the freezer

4 chicken legs or 8 drumsticks
50–75g (2–3oz) butter, onion salt
paprika
1 × 5ml tsp (1tsp) lemon juice
1 × 5ml tsp (1tsp) mixed, dried herbs
1 × 15ml tbsp (1tbsp) finely chopped parsley
salt

1 Dry chicken pieces well, Stir soft butter with ½ × 5ml tsp (½tsp) onion salt (or garlic salt), 1 × 5ml tsp (1tsp) paprika, lemon juice, herbs and parsley.

2 Brush chicken pieces with about ½ the spiced butter on one side, and place them with this side facing up in an ovenproof dish. Cover dish with tinfoil and leave in the bottom of the oven for about 20 min.

3 Remove tinfoil, turn chicken pieces and brush with the remaining butter. Sprinkle with a pinch of salt and replace dish in the middle of the oven, without the tinfoil. Leave oven door slightly ajar and baste chicken well with the butter.

Serve hot with a grinding of sea salt, and a potato salad or bread.

Chicken Pâté

(serves 6–8)
Preparation time: about 40 min
Cooking time: 1–1¼ hrs
Oven temperature: 200°C, 400°F, Gas 6
Suitable for the freezer

1 chicken
about 200g (7oz) calves' or chicken liver
1 small leek
3 sprigs of parsley
1 sprig of thyme
100g (4oz) bacon
50g (2oz) stuffed olives
100–200g (4–7oz) button mushrooms
butter, salt
pepper, lemon juice
1 × 15ml tbsp (1tbsp) port (optional)
For the mince: 250g (9oz) minced veal
salt, pepper, paprika
2 × 15ml tbsp (2tbsp) breadcrumbs
100ml (4fl oz) stock from chicken
2 eggs

1 Remove the meat from the chicken, discard skin, and slice. Simmer for about 15 min in a covered pan in about 200ml (7fl. oz) water with ½ × 5ml tsp (½tsp) salt, 4 black peppercorns and a small bouquet garni, consisting of the green part of the leek, parsley and thyme.

2 Sauté about ½ the bacon, cubed, until lightly golden, add 15g (½oz)

Above: Chicken Royale with sesame bread or rolls.

butter and sauté dried sliced liver quickly on both sides. Sprinkle with salt, black pepper and port.

3 Sauté whole, cleaned mushrooms for a couple of minutes in 15g (½oz) butter on high heat. Add salt to taste and squeeze the juice from ½ lemon on top.

4 To make the mince, mix veal with seasonings, breadcrumbs, strained stock from chicken, and eggs. Cut leek into thin rings and mix into the mince.

5 Grease a small pâté terrine or bread tin well with butter and layer in it, the mince, drained chicken meat, liver and bacon, sliced olives and mushrooms (with mince at top and bottom). Cover with remaining bacon rashers, place dish in a roasting tin half full of boiling water, and bake for about 1 hr.

6 Allow the pâté to cool completely before turning it out, or you can serve it straight from the dish.

Serve cold with bread, pickled gherkins and a green salad.

Snacks from Left-overs

The main ingredients in the following dishes are left-over cooked vegetables, fish and poultry.

Fish and Shrimp Cocottes
(above)
(serves 4)
Preparation time: about 15 min
Cooking time: 10–15 min
Oven temperature: 220°C, 425°F, Gas 7
Unsuitable for the freezer

*200–300g (7–11oz) cooked fish
  (skinned and boned)
100ml (4fl oz) sour or double cream
1 lemon*

*100–200g (4–7oz) peeled shrimps
100g (4oz) butter
1 shallot or small onion
1–2 cloves of garlic
1 sprig of parsley
2 slices of crustless white bread
salt, pepper
paprika*

1 Cut fish into bits and turn them in lightly whipped cream or sour cream, seasoned with lemon juice, salt, pepper and paprika. Place in small, greased, individual cocottes or ramekins with shrimps on top.
2 Stir soft butter with grated or finely chopped onion, crushed garlic, finely chopped parsley and crumbled bread. Sprinkle this mixture on top of shrimps and place dishes in the middle of the oven until baked through.

Vegetable Bake
(serves 4)
Preparation time: 15–20 min
Cooking time: 10–15 min
Oven temperature: 220–240°C, 425–475°F, Gas 7–9
Suitable for the freezer, but will lose flavour

*5–6 boiled, firm potatoes
a good quantity of left-over boiled
  vegetables
(carrots, green beans, peas,
  cauliflower, leeks etc)
2–3 onions
1–2 cloves of garlic
½ cucumber
50g (2oz) butter
1 sprig of parsley
rosemary, marjoram
salt, pepper
grated cheese (Cheddar or Gruyère)*

1 Chop vegetables into small pieces and place in a greased, ovenproof dish. Sprinkle with 2–3 × 15ml tbsp (2–3tbsp) grated cheese.

2 Cut cucumber into 1cm (½in) thick slices, then into strips. Sprinkle with salt.

Sauté chopped onions and crushed garlic in 15g (½oz) butter, but do not allow to go brown. Add slightly dried strips of cucumber and finely chopped parsley and leave to simmer for a couple of minutes. Season with salt, pepper and fresh or dried herbs, and pour onion mixture into dish. Season again to taste, and cover generously with grated cheese. Melt the remaining butter and drizzle over the top. Place dish in the middle of the oven until cheese is golden and vegetables are warmed through.

Serve with a fresh tomato salad. Thin slices of cold meat or fillets of smoked fish also go well with this dish.

Tomato Mousse with Chicken Salad

(serves 6)
Preparation time: 20–25 min
Cooling time: 3–4 hrs
Unsuitable for the freezer

25g (1oz) gelatine
200ml (7fl oz) hot, light stock
¼l (about 17fl oz) tomato juice
2 lemons
1–2 × 15ml tbsp (1–2tbsp) tomato purée
1 × 5ml tsp (1tsp) soy sauce
salt, pepper, nutmeg
150g (5oz) mayonnaise
1 × 5ml tsp (1tsp) Dijon mustard
300ml (½pt) sour cream
about 300g (11oz) cooked, sliced chicken meat
250g (9oz) mushrooms
1 small can of cut asparagus
cress, watercress, fresh basil or parsley

1 Dissolve gelatine in the hot stock (sprinkle gelatine *over* stock, not the other way round) stir quickly. Mix tomato juice with tomato purée and soy sauce and season with lemon juice, salt, pepper and nutmeg. Stir in melted gelatine and pour liquid into a ring mould which has been rinsed in cold water. Cover mould with tinfoil and put in a cold place, or in the refrigerator.

2 Mix together a sauce of mayonnaise, sour cream, lemon juice and/or asparagus juice from the can. Season with mustard, salt and pepper. Slice cleaned mushrooms thinly and add with cooked chicken to the sauce, together with well drained asparagus. Leave salad in a cold place for about 1 hr and season.

3 Turn tomato mousse out onto a serving dish. Put chicken salad into the hole in the middle, and garnish with cress, watercress, fresh basil or parsley. Bread, butter and lemon wedges are all that is needed to accompany this delicious dish.

Delicious Vegetable Bake made from an assortment of left-over vegetables.

Party Quiches

You don't always have to go to great lengths and great expense to make party food. Try this delicious quiche or one of its variations.

Crab and Asparagus Quiche
(serves 4–6)
Preparation time: 15–20 min
Cooling time for pastry: 1 hr
Baking time: about 30 min
Oven temperature: 180°C, 350°F, Gas 4
Unsuitable for the freezer

For the pastry : 100g (4oz) butter
175g (6oz) plain flour
3 × 15ml tbsp (3tbsp) water
For the filling : 1 can crab meat
1 can asparagus
salt, pepper
1–2 × 5ml tsp (1–2tsp) lemon juice
1 sprig of dill
For the soufflé : 2 egg whites
150g (5oz) mayonnaise

1 Rub pieces of cold butter and flour together with your fingertips until like breadcrumbs, and mix together with ice-cold water. Work quickly to a smooth dough, and leave in refrigerator for about 1 hr.
2 Roll out pastry, line flan dish and fill as shown and explained in the small pictures. Bake pie in the middle of the oven until base is crisp and surface is lightly golden and crisp.
Serve with a green salad.

TIPS
Quiches can be served with various kinds of fillings, not only the famous bacon and egg one. If filling is thin in consistency, you will get a better result if you prick the pastry well and then bake blind for 12–15 min at 200°C, 400°F, Gas 6, before adding filling to ensure a crisp base.

IDEAS FOR FILLINGS
Leek
Clean and slice 4 medium leeks into rings. Simmer for 6–8 min in 15g ($\frac{1}{2}$oz) butter, 100ml (4fl. oz) water and $\frac{1}{2}$ × 5ml tsp ($\frac{1}{2}$tsp) salt in a lidded pan. Place well drained leek rings in raw pastry case and sprinkle with a little grated nutmeg. Mix 100g (4oz) fresh cream cheese with a lightly beaten egg and 2 × 15ml tbsp (2tbsp) leek stock. Pour cheese

Crab and Asparagus Quiche

1 Good raw materials have been used in this delicious quiche. See below for alternate fillings.

2 Roll out pastry and press into flan dish. Prick bottom well with a fork.

3 Clean drained crab meat, remove any small bones and ligaments. Cut asparagus into bite-sized pieces.

4 Put filling into the pastry case, season, and sprinkle with finely chopped dill and lemon juice.

5 Whisk egg whites until peaks form and mix in the mayonnaise. Season with salt and pepper.

6 Spread soufflé mixture on top of quiche and bake for about 30 min at 180°C, 350°F, Gas 4.

cream over leeks and cover with 6–8 thin bacon rashers. Bake for about 30 min at 200°C, 400°F, Gas 6.

Chicken Liver

Fry 250–300g (9–11oz) dried chopped chicken livers for a couple of minutes. Sprinkle with salt and pepper. Sauté 2 finely chopped celery stalks and 250g (9oz) cleaned, sliced mushrooms in 25g (1oz) butter, with 1 × 15ml tbsp (1tbsp) lemon juice, salt and pepper. Thicken with 1 × 5ml tsp (1tsp) cornflour dissolved in 1 × 5ml tsp (1tsp) cold water or stock. Place chicken liver in pastry case which has been pre-baked for 12–15 min. Pour mushroom mixture over and sprinkle with about 50g (2oz) grated cheese. Bake at 220°C, 425°F, Gas 7, for 15–20 min.

Egg and Onion

Sauté 3–4 large, coarsely chopped onions until tender in 25g (1oz) butter. Turn off heat and stir in 100ml (4fl. oz) double cream, 4 lightly beaten eggs, 50–100 g (2–4oz) finely chopped cooked ham and some finely chopped chives. Season and pour filling into pre-baked pastry case. Bake at 200°C, 400°F, Gas 6, for 15–20 min.

Tasty Weekend Supper

Weekends are for relaxing, and enjoying life. The following recipes are tasty and easy to prepare.

Tomato Quiche with Rosemary

(below)
(serves 4–6)
Preparation time: 10–15 min
Cooling time for pastry: 1 hr
Cooking time: 25–30 min
Oven temperature: 200°C, 400°F, Gas 6
Suitable for the freezer, but will lose flavour

quiche pastry (see page 46)
For the filling : 2 onions
15g (½oz) butter
1 clove of garlic
salt, pepper
2 × 15ml tbsp (2tbsp) tomato purée
100–150g (4–5oz) cooked meat
4–6 ripe tomatoes
rosemary, basil
2–3 × 15ml tbsp (2–3tbsp) grated Parmesan cheese
about 100g (4oz) mild, grated cheese

1 Make pastry as explained on page 46, and leave in a cold place for at least 1 hr.
2 Roll out pastry and line a flan tin. Prick the bottom with a fork and bake base blind for 10–15 min.
3 Sauté coarsely chopped onions in butter until shiny. Add crushed garlic, tomato purée, coarsely chopped meat and seasonings to taste.
3 Fill pie base with mixture, and cover with overlapping tomato slices. Sprinkle with salt, pepper and grated Parmesan and finally fresh or dried rosemary and basil.

4 Cover everything with a layer of grated mild cheese and bake in the middle of the oven for 10–20 min until cheese has melted and is light gold in colour.
Serve warm with a simple salad.

Cheese and Tomato Bake

(serves 4)
Preparation time: about 10 min
Cooking time: 35 min
Oven temperature: 220°C, 425°F, Gas 7
Unsuitable for the freezer

8 crustless slices of white bread
4 large tomatoes
8 thick slices of cheese (Gruyère or Emmenthal)
2 eggs
400ml (¾pt) milk
salt, pepper
1 × 5ml tsp (1tsp) crushed rosemary
1 × 5ml tsp (1tsp) made mustard
butter

1 Grease a large ovenproof dish. Butter white bread slices thinly and place close together in the dish. Place cheese and half a tomato on each slice.

2 Whisk eggs, milk, salt, pepper, rosemary and mustard together lightly and pour into the dish. Bake in oven until egg mixture is stiff and lightly golden.

Neapolitan Pizza (right)

(serves 4–6)
Preparation time: about 20 min
Rising time: 15–20 min
Cooking time: about 15–20 min
Oven temperature: 220–240°C, 425–475°F, Gas 7–9
Freeze raw, with or without filling

For the dough : 225g (8oz) plain
flour
1 × 5ml tsp (1tsp) salt
8g (¼oz) fresh yeast or 1 × 5ml tsp
(1tsp) dried
¼ × 5ml tsp (¼tsp) sugar
150ml (¼pt) warm water
1 × 15ml tbsp (1tbsp) oil
For the topping : 2 × 15ml tbsp
(2tbsp) oil
1 small can tomato purée
about 700g (1½lb) ripe tomatoes
2 onions, 1–2 cloves of garlic
50–100g (2–4oz) mushrooms
15–20 black and green olives
100g (4oz) ham or salami or 1 can
anchovy fillets
1–2 × 15ml tbsp (1–2tbsp) capers
salt, pepper, paprika
basil, marjoram, rosemary, thyme
about 150g (5oz) cheese (Cheddar,
Mozzarella or Gruyère)

1 Sieve flour and salt into a bowl, and blend fresh yeast with warm water. If using dried yeast, dissolve sugar in warm water, sprinkle on yeast, and leave to get frothy in a warm place. Add yeast mixture to flour along with oil. Mix to a soft dough then knead until smooth and elastic. Leave in bowl, covered, to double in size.

2 Meanwhile make the filling. Mix tomato purée with ½ the oil, crushed garlic and seasonings. Wash tomatoes, peel onions and mushrooms. Cut mushrooms and olives into slices (remove stones if any). Cut ham or salami into thin strips or drain anchovy fillets.

3 Pat out dough to make a large circular shape. Place on a greased baking sheet. Fold a small edge all around the edges of the dough. Spread tomato purée on top, arrange the other topping ingredients over as in the picture, and sprinkle with spices and fresh or dried herbs.

4 Cut cheese into slices and place on top of pizza topping. Sprinkle with remaining oil and bake in the middle of the oven until dough is crisp, the filling hot and the cheese golden. Serve straight from the oven with a green salad.

VARIATIONS
Tuna Fish Topping

1 can tuna fish in oil, well drained
4–5 ripe tomatoes, sliced
½ green pepper, sliced into rings
10 stoneless black olives
salt, pepper
paprika, oil
marjoram, basil
lemon balm
100g (4oz) mild, grated cheese
(Mozzarella or Gruyère)

Salami Topping:

1 can tomato purée
4–5 ripe tomatoes, sliced
1 chopped onion, 1 crushed garlic
clove
100g (4oz) salami, first thinly
sliced, then chopped
10 stuffed olives, sliced
salt, pepper, paprika
oil, chives, marjoram, basil
12–14 slices Mozzarella or Gruyère
cheese

From the Frying Pan

If you are occasionally landed with unexpected hungry guests, make sure you always have some eggs handy. Omelettes and scrambled eggs combine with other ingredients in many different, tasty, and filling ways.

French Omelette

(serves 2–4)
Preparation time: about 5 min
Cooking time: 2–3 min
Unsuitable for the freezer

4 eggs, salt, pepper
butter
4 × 15ml tbsp (4tbsp) cream or water

1 Whisk eggs lightly together with cream or water, salt and pepper.
2 Heat frying or omelette pan well, add 15–25g ($\frac{1}{2}$–1oz) butter, and pour egg mixture into pan when butter has stopped simmering or has

Eggs and tomatoes go well together, here pictured with shrimps and fresh herbs.

slightly browned.

3 Move a fork or a wooden spatula backwards and forwards along the bottom of the pan. Shake it a little to make sure the liquid mixture covers the bottom. When the entire omelette has almost set (after about 1–2 min), leave for about 1 min to set further and brown on the bottom.

Now add the warm filling, if you are not serving a plain omelette.

Shrimp Omelette with Tomatoes

(serves 4)
Preparation time: about 10 min
Cooking time: about 25 min in all
Unsuitable for the freezer

1 basic French omelette mixture (see above)
4 × 15ml tbsp (4tbsp) finely chopped fresh herbs (parsley, chives, chervil)
about 200g (7oz) peeled shrimps
1 onion, 40–50g (1½–2oz) butter
1 clove of garlic
1 can tomatoes
salt, pepper, marjoram
1 lemon

Rice Omelette can be made from left-overs, and is filling as well as delicious.

1 Sauté finely chopped onion in 15g (½oz) butter, add drained tomatoes and crushed garlic. Leave tomato sauce to simmer uncovered for about 20 min until thick and smooth. Season with salt, pepper and a touch of dried marjoram.

2 Heat shrimps in 15g (½oz) butter, a touch of lemon juice and salt. Do not allow to boil.

3 Mix finely chopped, green herbs into omelette mixture and fry as explained in previous recipe. Add ½ the shrimps to the tomato sauce, pour over omelette when nearly ready. Drop the rest of the shrimps on top and sprinkle with some finely chopped parsley or chives.

Serve immediately with warm French bread and butter.

Rice Omelette

(serves 4)
Preparation time: 10–15 min
Cooking time: about 15 min
Unsuitable for the freezer

1 basic French omelette mixture (see previous page)
1 onion, 25–40g (1–1½oz) butter
about 150g (5oz) thin frankfurter, chorizo or cabanos sausages
100ml (4fl oz) stock
a pinch of cayenne pepper
about 50g (2oz) boiled rice
4–6 small, ripe tomatoes
salt, pepper, paprika
1 bunch of chives

1 Sauté finely chopped onion and sausage slices in about ½ the butter and pour over some stock mixed with the cayenne pepper. Add rice and tomato wedges and heat well. Sprinkle with a pinch of salt and pepper, and paprika over the tomatoes.
2 In a separate omelette or frying pan, fry omelette until nearly ready, then place rice filling on top. Cook for a further min and sprinkle with chives.
Serve with bread and a green salad.

Shellfish Omelette

(serves 4)
Preparation time: about 20 min
Cooking time: about 10 min in all
Unsuitable for the freezer

1 basic French omelette mixture (see previous page)
1 avocado, 1 lemon
2 × 15ml tbsp (2tbsp) tomato purée
salt, pepper
paprika
1 can mussels
200g (7oz) peeled shrimps

1 Squeeze lemon juice into a small bowl. Halve avocado, and remove peel and stone. Cut flesh into small slices straight into the lemon juice, and sprinkle with some salt and white pepper. Stir carefully to cover all the flesh with juice (to prevent discolouration).
2 Heat mussels and shrimps in juices from mussel can. Do *not* boil.
3 Stir tomato purée and ½ × 5ml tsp (½tsp) paprika into basic omelette mixture and fry just until it has begun to set. Add avocado, lemon juice, and drained shellfish. Cover the pan for a few minutes, to allow avocado to warm through.
Serve with toast, butter and lemon wedges.

Above: Shellfish Omelette has an unusual combination of shrimps, mussels and avocado.
Below: Scrambled Eggs with finely chopped onions and smoked boiling sausage.

Scrambled Eggs with Ham and Shrimps and a dash of curry powder which adds flavour and colour.

Scrambled Eggs

Preparation time: about 5 min
Cooking time: 3–5 min
Unsuitable for the freezer

4 eggs, salt, white pepper
1 × 15ml tbsp (1 tbsp) cream
15g (½oz) butter

1 Whisk eggs lightly with the seasonings and cream. Heat butter in a heavy-bottomed frying pan or non-stick saucepan over low heat. Do not allow butter to brown.
2 Pour in egg and scrape along the edges with a wooden spatula as the mixture sets. When soft and creamy it is ready. Place on a hot dish.
NOTE: Do not allow the eggs to scramble for too long, as they will be dry and watery. Salt can also draw the liquid out of scrambled eggs, so it might be advisable to add salt just before it has finished cooking.

Scrambled Eggs with Ham and Shrimps

(serves 4)
Preparation time: about 10 min
Cooking time: 8–10 min
Unsuitable for the freezer

1 basic scrambled egg mixture (see previous recipe)
100g (4oz) cooked ham
15–25g (½–1oz) butter
about 100g (4oz) peeled shrimps
½ lemon, ½–1 × 5ml tsp (½–1 tsp) curry powder
3 × 15ml tbsp (3 tbsp) finely chopped parsley

1 Coarsely chop ham into small cubes. Heat for a couple of min in butter in a saucepan or frying pan with a thick bottom. Add peeled shrimps and lemon juice and allow everything to heat through gently and thoroughly.
2 Whisk curry powder into plain scrambled egg mixture and pour over the ham and shrimps. Scrape along the bottom with a wooden spatula until the mixture starts to set. Sprinkle with parsley.

Serve on butter-fried slices of bread, with wedges of lemon.

Scrambled Eggs with Sausages

(serves 4)
Preparation time: 5–10 min
Cooking time: 8–10 min in all
Unsuitable for the freezer

1 basic scrambled egg mixture (see left)
2 shallots or small onions
15–25g (½–1oz) butter
4 thin frankfurters (or other boiling sausage)
1 × 5ml tsp (1 tsp) Dijon mustard

1 Sauté finely chopped onions and sausage slices in butter over medium heat.
2 Whisk mustard into the egg mixture and pour over onion and sausages. Scrape mixture along the bottom of the saucepan with a wooden spatula until eggs have set slightly.
Serve with rolls or toast and butter, and sprinkle with chopped chives if you like.

53

Bread with a Difference

Homemade bread is always tasty. On the following pages you will find recipes using various types of loaf.

Homemade Bread

Preparation time: about 15 min
Rising time: 1–1¼ hrs in all
Baking time: about 35 min
Oven temperature: 200–220°C, 400–425°F, Gas 6–7
Suitable for the freezer

25g (1oz) fresh yeast or 15g (½oz) dried
200ml (7fl oz) warm water
100ml (4fl oz) milk or buttermilk
1–2 × 5ml tsp (1–2tsp) salt
2 × 15ml tbsp (2tbsp) oil or melted butter

about 500g (1lb 2oz) strong plain flour

1 Dissolve fresh yeast in warm water and add milk, salt, butter or oil and most of the flour. If using dried yeast, dissolve ½ × 5ml tsp (½tsp) sugar in warm water, sprinkle on yeast, and leave to get frothy in a warm place. Then proceed as for fresh yeast. Work dough well, use more flour if necessary, until soft, smooth and elastic. Allow dough to rise, covered, in a warm place until twice its size (about 1 hr).

2 Place dough on a surface sprinkled with flour, knead and shape to make an oblong or round loaf, or whatever shape you fancy. Leave to rise on a greased baking sheet for 20 min more.

3 Slash or decorate the top of the loaf in some way, if you like, and brush with water, milk, cream or whisked egg. Sprinkle with poppy seeds, sesame seeds, cracked wheat, nuts etc. Bake as indicated and place bread to cool on a wire rack. The bread is cooked when you tap the bottom of the loaf and it sounds hollow, like a drum.

NOTE: If you prefer a coarser bread, use one half plain flour and the rest a mixture of wholemeal and rye flour, perhaps.

Bread Ring with Cheese Cream

(serves 6–8)
Preparation time for filling: about 15 min
Suitable for the freezer, but will deteriorate somewhat in flavour

1 basic home-made bread dough, made with ½ rye or wholemeal flour
For the filling : 200g (7oz) cottage cheese
50g (2oz) grated cheese (Gruyère or Cheddar)
cream

1–2 pickled red peppers
2 pickled gherkins
1 bunch of chives and/or parsley
salt, pepper, caraway seeds

1 Make 1 portion basic bread dough, but use about 200g (7oz) rye or wholemeal flour in place of plain, and leave to double in size.
2 Knead dough well, divide and roll out to make two long shapes. Twist these rolls around each other, shape into a ring, and leave on a baking sheet to rise again. Make small slashes around the ring, brush with water or milk, and bake for about 30 min (see basic recipe).
3 Mix cottage cheese until smooth with a little cream, and stir in grated cheese, very finely chopped pepper, gherkins and chives or parsley. If necessary, stir in more cream until smooth, but not too thin, in consistency. Season with salt, pepper and caraway.
4 Slice the cooled bread ring in two and spread cheese cream over cut surfaces. Leave ring for a while in a cool place (*not* the refrigerator), before slicing and serving.
Serve with a green salad or crisp stalks of celery.

Left: Homemade bread baked in a
ring and filled with a delicious
cheese cream. Above: Spicy Ham
Bread with salad – tasty and
filling for lunch or supper.

Spicy Ham Bread
(serves 6–8)
Preparation time for filling: about 15 min
Heating time: 10–15 min
Oven temperature: 220°C, 425°F, Gas 7
Suitable for the freezer

1 long loaf (homemade, see recipe, or
*   bought)*
For the filling: about 100g (4oz)
*   butter*
1 shallot or small onion
1 clove of garlic
2–3 × 5ml tsp (2–3tsp) Dijon
*   mustard*
1–2 × 5ml tsp (1–2tsp) lemon juice
200–300g (7–11oz) cooked ham or
*   smoked pork*
2–3 pickled gherkins
1 sprig of parsley

1 Slice the cool bread, but do not cut all the way through. It should still be attached at the bottom.
2 Mix soft butter, grated onion, crushed garlic, mustard and lemon juice together. Cut meat and gherkins into tiny cubes and stir into butter with finely chopped parsley.
3 Spread mixture well down between slices, squeeze lightly together and wrap bread in tin foil, but leave open at the top. Heat bread in oven as indicated.
Serve with a bowl of crisp salad and French dressing.

VARIATIONS
Curried Egg Filling
Mix 200g (7oz) mayonnaise with 2–3 × 15ml tbsp (2–3tbsp) curry powder, juice from 1 lemon and 100ml (4fl. oz) cream or sour cream. Mix in 4–6 hard-boiled, chopped eggs, some cleaned and finely chopped green pepper, and a generous amount of finely chopped cress. Season with salt and pepper. If you use this filling, do not heat bread and do not freeze.
A fresh tomato salad with lemon or an oil and vinegar dressing is a delicious accompaniment.

Sardine Rolls
(serves 6)
Preparation time for filling: about 20 min
Baking time with filling: about 10 min at 220–240°C, 425–475°F, Gas 7–9
Suitable for the freezer, but will lose flavour

1 basic homemade bread dough with
*   wheatmeal flour (see page 54) or 6*
*   large brown rolls*
For the filling: 2 cans of sardines in
*   oil*
2 lemons, salt, pepper
50g (2oz) stuffed olives
4 eggs
1 tomato
6 × 15ml tbsp (6tbsp) mild, grated
*   cheese Cheddar or Gruyère)*

Above : Homemade or bought rolls can be filled with a variety of good things – here sardines, olives, eggs and tomato.
Right : A different way of using French Bread – an open sandwich that goes on for ever !

1 Make basic dough with 100–200g (4–7oz) wheatmeal flour replacing same quantity of plain flour. Leave to rise until double in size. Shape dough into 6 large rounds. Leave to rise again for a further 15–20 min on a baking sheet, and brush with cream or beaten egg. Bake for 15–20 min in the middle of the oven.
2 Cut a lid off the cooled rolls and scrape out most of the inside dough. (Dry the unused lids in the oven and crush to make breadcrumbs.) Place inside dough in a bowl and add oil from sardines, juice of $\frac{1}{2}$ lemon, 2 lightly beaten eggs and seasonings to taste.
3 Divide about $\frac{1}{2}$ the above filling between the excavated rolls. Place pieces of boneless sardines and sliced olives on top and sprinkle with a little lemon juice.
4 Hard-boil the remaining 2 eggs, chop them up and mix with the bread-filling left. Spread the mixture evenly over the top of the rolls and sprinkle with grated cheese. Bake rolls in oven until cheese melts and is light gold in colour. Garnish with tomato wedges, and serve with a green salad.

French Bread
(makes 2–3)
Preparation time : 15–20 min
Rising time : $2\frac{1}{2}$ hrs
Cooking time : 12–15 min
Oven temperature : 240°C, 475°F, Gas 9, or higher if possible
Suitable for the freezer

25g (1oz) fresh yeast or 15g ($\frac{1}{2}$oz) dried
300ml ($\frac{1}{2}$pt) warm water
2 × 5ml tsp (2tsp) salt
1 × 15ml tbsp (1tbsp) oil
about 500g (1lb 2oz) strong plain flour

1 Dissolve crumbled fresh yeast in warm water, add salt, oil and most of the flour. Work the dough well, and knead in the remaining flour until smooth and elastic. Leave to rise for 2 hrs in a warm place. If using dried yeast dissolve sugar in warm water, then add yeast, stir, and leave to become frothy in a warm place. Then proceed as for fresh yeast.
2 Remove to a floured board, knead again, and cut into 2–3 pieces. Shape into balls, and allow to rest for 4–5 min before you roll them out to form long, thick sausages. Place, covered, on greased baking sheet for a further rising of about $\frac{1}{2}$ hr. Brush with lightly salted, tepid water and make 2–3 long z-shaped cuts on top.
3 Put a little ovenproof cup of warm water in the bottom of the oven, and bake as indicated. Brush French loaf with water while baking for a really crisp crust. Cool on a rack.

French Bread with Meat Filling
(serves 6–8)
Preparation time for filling : about 20 min
Baking time : about 20 min
Oven temperature : 220°C, 425°F, Gas 7
Suitable for the freezer before baking

2 French loaves, bought or home-made
butter, salt, pepper
paprika
about 400g (14oz) minced beef or pork
2 onions, 1 egg
1 × 15ml tbsp (1tbsp) breadcrumbs
1 × 15ml tbsp (1tbsp) tomato purée
1 × 15ml tbsp (1tbsp) mustard
2 green peppers
4 tomatoes
8 slices Gruyère or Emmenthal cheese

1 Slice French loaves lengthwise and butter the flat surfaces. Mix mince with spices, grated or finely chopped onion, egg, breadcrumbs, tomato purée and mustard.
2 Place meat in an even layer on loaves and place on baking sheet. Sprinkle with about 2 × 15ml tbsp (2tbsp) melted butter and bake for about 15 min in the middle of the oven.
3 Cut cleaned pepper into thin rings and tomatoes into slices. Place on filling and spread cheese sticks on top as in illustration. Place loaves in oven until cheese has begun to melt.

Exciting Rice Dishes

Chinese Fried Rice (right)
(serves 4)
Preparation time: about 15 min
Cooking time: 20–25 min
Unsuitable for the freezer

175g (6oz) long-grain rice
salt, oil, butter
500ml (just under 1pt) stock
2 carrots
1 green pepper
2 stalks of celery
2 shallots or small onions
salt, pepper
100–200g (4–7oz) mushrooms
½ can beansprouts or about 50g
* (2oz) fresh*
½–1 × 15ml tbsp (½–1tbsp) soy sauce

1 Sauté rice in 2 × 15ml tbsp (2tbsp) oil on low heat. Add 1 × 5ml tsp (1tsp) salt and 400ml (¾pt) stock, stir well and simmer for 18–20 min, covered.
2 Clean vegetables and cut up. Cook carrot slices for 10 min in 1 × 15ml tbsp (1tbsp) butter and remaining stock. Add finely chopped celery, pepper and onion rings, cook for a further 2 min, and place mushroom slices and beansprouts in pan. Bring to the boil and season with soy sauce, salt and pepper.
3 Stir the rice carefully with a fork, and pour vegetables and meat juices over it.
Serve with a few slices of roast beef, chicken or turkey meat.

Italian Risotto with Fish
(above)
(serves 4)
Preparation time: about 15 min
Cooking time: 20–25 min
Unsuitable for the freezer

1 onion, 1 green pepper
2 × 15ml tbsp (2tbsp) oil
1 clove of garlic

175g (6oz) long-grained rice
400ml (¾pt) stock
salt, pepper
fresh or dried tarragon
250–300g (9–11oz) cooked fillets of
    cod or other firm fish
1 lemon
10–12 black olives
1 can mussels
fresh dill

1 Sauté chopped onion and cleaned, sliced pepper for a couple of minutes in oil. Add crushed garlic and rice, stir carefully, and leave on the heat until the rice is slightly golden.
2 Keep back about 50ml (2fl. oz) stock and add rest to the rice in the pan, along with salt and pepper. Sprinkle with a little fresh, finely chopped tarragon or a pinch of crushed dried, and simmer for 18–20 min under a tight-fitting lid.
3 Heat well drained mussels, flaked fish fillets, and sliced, black stoneless olives in the remaining stock and add a touch of lemon juice. Stir the cooked rice with a fork and transfer to a hot serving dish. Put fish mixture on top and garnish with sprigs of dill.
Serve hot with hard-boiled eggs and a green salad.

Southern Jambalaya with Sausages (above)
(serves 4–6)
Preparation time: about 20 min
Cooking time: about 20 min
Unsuitable for the freezer

1–2 onions, 2 cloves of garlic
3 × 15ml tbsp (3tbsp) olive oil
2 stalks of celery
1 green pepper
175g (6oz) long-grain rice
500ml (just under 1pt) chicken stock
1 × 15ml tbsp (1tbsp) tomato purée
salt, pepper, paprika
200g (1oz) cooked ham
about 300g (11oz) sausages,
    preferably garlic flavoured
4 ripe tomatoes
200g (7oz) peeled shrimps
marjoram, thyme, parsley

1 Sauté chopped onion and crushed garlic for a few minutes in 2 × 15ml tbsp (2tbsp) olive oil. Add sliced celery, cleaned and chopped pepper and the rice. Stir carefully, add 400 ml (¾pt) stock, tomato purée and spices. Simmer under tight-fitting lid for about 15 min on low heat.
2 Cut ham into cubes and sausages into slices. Sauté in remaining oil. Scald and peel tomatoes, cut into four and mix in with ham and sausage. Add remaining stock and bring to the boil. Heap peeled shrimps into the mixture, but do not allow to boil. Season generously with salt, pepper and herbs.
3 Lift the cooked rice from time to time with a fork, then transfer to a deep serving dish, and keep warm. Add meat and shrimps and mix everything together lightly with two wooden forks (to allow the various tastes to mingle). Sprinkle with finely chopped parsley, and serve immediately, with a salad.
NOTE: Well spiced, grilled or baked chicken can be used instead of sausages.

Exciting Pasta Dishes

Pasta dishes include spaghetti, macaroni, tagliatelli, lasagne, cannelloni, vermicelli and numerous other varieties. Pasta is made from a hard wheat flour to which is added oil and water, and sometimes eggs and spinach. Only small quantities of meat are used in pasta dishes, or they are made without adding meat at all, which therefore makes it both economical and filling. All pasta is boiled, but the time varies according to size and shape It should be cooked until al dente, when it is just firm to the bite.

Cooking Pasta

Allow roughly 75–100g (3–4oz) macaroni, noodles or spaghetti per person, according to appetite, the amount of sauce and other accompaniments served, or whether a starter or main course. Bring about 500ml (1pt) water per 50g (2oz) pasta to the boil and add 1–2 × 5ml tsp (1–2tsp) salt. Put pasta in water and simmer on medium heat with the lid half on.

The cooking time depends, as above, on the thickness of the pasta. Roughly speaking, noodles or tagliatelle need 10 min, spaghetti 10–12 min. To test, bite a piece; it should have a little firmness.

Pour pasta into a sieve or colander and leave to drain. Add 1 × 15ml tbsp (1tbsp) butter or oil to the dry, hot saucepan, and return pasta to the saucepan. Toss thoroughly over a strong heat.

Pasta which is to be served warm should never be rinsed in cold water. It will then stick together when you heat it up again. If the boiling water appears gluey, there was not enough water in the first place.

Tagliatelle with Ham Sauce

(left)

(serves 4)

Preparation time: about 10 min
Cooking time: about 20 min in all
Unsuitable for the freezer

350–450g (¾–1lb) white or green
    tagliatelle (noodles)
250ml (9fl oz) cream
1 leek
2 egg yolks
about 50–75g (2–3oz) grated cheese
    (Cheddar, Gruyère)
½–1 × 5ml tsp (½–1tsp) dried herbs
salt, pepper, nutmeg
150–200g (5–7oz) cooked ham
about 50g (2oz) small, frozen peas
½ sprig finely chopped parsley

1 Boil noodles until *al dente* and keep warm. Bring cream with cleaned, finely chopped leek to the boil. Remove saucepan from heat and stir in the egg yolks.

2 Place saucepan on very low heat and stir in grated cheese until it melts. The sauce must *not* boil. Mix in small cubes of ham and peas and season to taste with salt, pepper, nutmeg and herbs.

3 Place noodles into a large warm bowl or individual warm bowls. Pour sauce over and sprinkle with finely chopped parsley.
Serve with tomato salad, and hand grated Parmesan cheese separately.

Tagliatelle with Walnut Sauce (above)

(serves 4)

Preparation time: about 15 min
Cooking time: about 20 min in all
Unsuitable for the freezer

350–450g (¾–1lb) green or white
    tagliatelli (noodles)
250g (9oz) mushrooms
15–25g (½–1oz) butter
1 × 15ml tbsp (1tbsp) plain flour
½ lemon
300–400ml (½–¾pt) stock
salt, pepper, parsley
50–100g (2–4oz) walnut kernels

1 Boil noodles until *al dente*, and keep warm.

2 Sauté peeled, sliced mushrooms for a couple of minutes in butter, sprinkle with flour and stir in with stock and lemon juice. Bring to the boil, stirring continuously; season.

3 Coarsely chop up walnuts and add these and finely chopped parsley to the sauce. Allow to cook for 1 min and add a touch more salt if necessary. Place spaghetti on a hot serving dish and pour the sauce over.

Spaghetti with Liver Sauce
(serves 4)
Preparation time: about 10 min
Cooking time: about 15 min in all
The liver sauce can be frozen

350–450g (¾–1lb) spaghetti
200–300g (7–11oz) calves' liver
2 onions
2 cooking apples
50–100g (2–4oz) bacon
25g (1oz) butter
200–300ml (7–10fl oz) stock
250ml (¼pt) red wine (optional)
salt, black pepper, nutmeg
thyme, rosemary
cornflour

1 Cook spaghetti *al dente* (see page 61) and keep warm. Slice peeled onions into thin rings and peeled apples into wedges.
2 Brown small bacon cubes and drain on fat-absorbent paper. Pour most of the bacon fat out of the pan, add ½ the butter and fry small, dried liver slices on both sides on strong heat. Season and remove liver from the pan with a slotted spoon.
3 Add the rest of the butter to pan, fry onion rings and apple wedges on low heat, then add stock and red wine, if used. Simmer on low heat for about 5 min. Place bacon and liver into sauce, and allow to simmer for 3–4 min. Season with salt, pepper, nutmeg and fresh or dried herbs. Thicken sauce with a little cornflour dissolved in cold water. Place spaghetti on a hot dish or dishes and pour liver sauce over. Serve with grated Parmesan cheese and a green salad.

Spaghetti Bolognese
(serves 4)
Preparation time: about 15 min
Cooking time: 20–30 min in all
The meat sauce can be frozen

350–450g (¾–1lb) spaghetti
For the sauce : 2 onions, 1 clove of
    garlic
50g (2oz) bacon, 2 × 15ml tbsp
    (2tbsp) oil
250g (9oz) pork or beef mince
1 celery stalk
1 carrot, 1 bay leaf
½ red or green pepper
1 can tomatoes
1 small can tomato purée
salt, pepper, paprika
100g (4oz) mushrooms
150ml (¼pt) red wine (optional)
4 × 15ml tbsp (4tbsp) sour cream

1 Start with the meat sauce. Sauté coarsely chopped onions, crushed garlic and small bacon cubes in oil. Add mince and stir on strong heat until meat looks like breadcrumbs and changes colour.
2 Turn heat down and stir in very finely chopped celery and pepper, grated carrot, tinned tomatoes, bay-leaf and tomato purée. Allow sauce to simmer for 15–20 min and stir from time to time. Put water in a saucepan and place on cooker. Boil spaghetti until *al dente* (see page 61).
3 Add cleaned, sliced mushrooms, red wine and seasonings to the sauce. Allow to cook for a few more minutes.
Place spaghetti on a hot dish or dishes and pour meat sauce over. Place small dollops of sour cream on top.

Pictured right is the classic Italian spaghetti – with Bolognese Sauce – but why not try the more unusual Liver Sauce below?

Index